BRIT-BRIT!
You Dress Me NICE!

TRUE TALES FROM THE WORLD OF SPORTSCASTING

ANCHORBOY

JAY ONRAIT

Collins

HarperCollins Publishers Ltd

2 Bloor Street East, 20th Floor

Toronto, Ontario, Canada

M4W 1A8

www.harpercollins.ca

Library and Archives Canada Cataloguing in Publication

Onrait, Jay, author

Anchorboy : true tales from the world of sportscasting / Jay Onrait.

ISBN 978-1-44342-947-4

Printed and bound in the United States of America

RRD 9 8 7 6 5 4 3 2 1

For my parents

CONTENTS

FOREWORD

I AM ACTUALLY VERY SURPRISED you are reading this right now. Shocked, even. Jay still hasn't returned my daughter's copy of *Bee Movie*, yet he managed to write a book. My kids sure did like that movie. I guess I will have to read them this book in its place. I hope it has plenty of stories involving bees.

I have spent a lot of time with this man. I mean a lot. Yet somehow we don't hate each other. Still, after eleven years of working together, when Jay sees me or calls me, he insists on saying, no matter where we are, in a very loud broadcaster-like voice, "Hi, Dan! I'm Jay Onrait. Remember, we work together?" It is odd.

Odd things happen when I am with Jay. We were in Sudbury, Ontario, for a speaking engagement. I checked in to our hotel and was getting changed when I heard a key in my door. Because of a mix-up at the front desk, that key was held by Jay Onrait, who opened the door to reveal me standing in a towel and nothing more. So did he quickly close the door and leave like any other human would do? Of course not. We made love. Kidding. Seriously. We didn't. What Jay did do was proceed to have a chat with me about a cheese plate he saw on a desk in my room. Where did it come from? Did I order it? How did it get there so quickly? Could he have some? Again, it was odd.

Odd . . . That's probably the best way to sum up this book, which means it will be a great read. I owe this man everything for where our partnership has taken us, so the least I could do was write this horrible, horrible foreword.

Here's hoping the rest of the book is better than this slop.

Enjoy, and thanks for laughing along with us for all those years!

Dan O'Toole

P.S. I highly recommend *Bee Movie*.

CHAPTER 1

The Full-Body Unitard

A FULL-BODY UNITARD is a sight to behold. Nothing is left to the imagination. When a man puts on a full-body unitard, it's either going to be extremely flattering or extremely disappointing. Guess which category I fall into?

During the final days of the 2012 Summer Olympic Games in London, England, Nicole Anderson, our production manager at TSN, went out and purchased a full-body unitard. It was just like the ones the "Green Men" wear to harass opposing players who sit in the penalty box at Vancouver Canucks games. Only instead of a green unitard, Nicole found a blue unitard with a large Union Jack on the front. It was pretty spectacular. I knew I wanted to use it for some sort of funny story with me harassing locals or tourists at an Olympic venue or out in the street. That's probably what I should have done. Instead I decided to take it one step further and see if I could catch the attention of NBC Olympic broadcasters outside their cafeteria. It was an old-school Letterman-style segment I cleverly titled "Greeting People Outside the NBC Olympic Cafeteria."

I thought it covered all the bases: If we were blown off by anchors or, more likely, their PR people, we could use it in the segment because that would be part of the fun, but we'd still have them on camera and very likely get more high-profile people that way. At the same time we wouldn't have to do an elaborate set-up with a tripod and lighting; we could just shoot it guerilla style. And then of course there was the pure visual absurdity of a six-foot-five sports anchor dressed in a full-body unitard with a Union Jack. Surely if we were turned down by every NBC personality we saw, we would still get a few appreciative laughs from some of them. I thought it was a pretty fun idea, but not everyone has the same definition of "fun" that I do.

It all started well: I rode the Tube to the Olympic Park wearing the full-body unitard. I paid my fare, walked down the escalator into London's depths, and walked onto a crowded train. I also donned fake Ray-Bans with a Union Jack design to complete the look. The "look" got plenty of looks on London public transit and then drew even more attention at Olympic Park. I even had to stop and pose for pictures in the London 2012 Megastore. After sweltering in the outfit for a couple of hours at the BMX track, I made my way to the International Broadcast Centre once again and met my camera guy for the segment, Dave Parker. Dave grew up in Onoway, Alberta, not far from Athabasca, Alberta, where I grew up. Both towns were practically identical: agricultural centres of fewer than 3,000 people in the middle of the prairies. I had spent plenty of weekends in my youth in Onoway playing minor hockey, probably against Dave, and he was the epitome of a "good Alberta boy." This was going to be fun!

Before Dave arrived, I was standing next to the cafeteria in the full-body unitard when NBC NFL play-by-play legend Al Michaels strolled by. "Al!" I called out. I had briefly met him while covering the 2004 NBA Finals in San Antonio, which he called for NBC, but he wouldn't have remembered me in a suit, much less a unitard. Still, he was extremely gracious for such an industry heavyweight and looked to be considering my request for "a quick interview," only to have his PR vulture swoop in and whisk him away. PR people had been the bane of my existence at these Games, and this was no exception. No matter, I had my routine down. Dave arrived and we got to work.

Suddenly emerging from the cafeteria was tennis legend and bad boy extraordinaire John McEnroe. He actually noticed us before we noticed him and smirked.

"Johnny Mac! Quick interview?" I pleaded. Again, keep in mind I was wearing a skin-tight spandex outfit.

"Maybe later," he replied, which easily translated to "I hope I never have to see you or that outfit ever again." He walked by later and chatted with me briefly as I walked alongside him, Dave rolling the camera as I tried unsuccessfully to get him to stop. The whole time McEnroe had a smile on his face, never seeming truly agitated, and this is a guy who is known for always being agitated. He was a good sport about the whole thing, and his reaction was exactly what I was looking for. I turned around to Dave and said, "That was awesome!"

"It was?" he replied. "Okay then!"

Then, like a vision, former ESPN *SportsNation* co-host Michelle Beadle emerged from the NBC Olympic cafeteria with a Pret A Manger sandwich in her hand. Like me, she was much more beautiful in person than she appeared on television. Michelle had just joined NBC to co-host *Access Hollywood* alongside Billy Bush as well as provide sports coverage for various NBC properties. The Olympics were essentially her first NBC gig. The fact that she was also a former ESPN personality and her show had appeared on TSN2 for the past couple of years was also a nice tie-in for our own network. But that wasn't the real reason she was so perfect for the segment. She was perfect for the segment because she stopped and talked to me. We had a very brief conversation that went something like this:

ONRAIT: How are the Games going?

BEADLE: Great, great!

ONRAIT: Happy to be working for NBC?

BEADLE: Yes, very happy to be living in New York.

ONRAIT: So that means you're happy to no longer be living in Bristol? [Connecticut, much-maligned small-town home of ESPN]

BEADLE: Yes, New York is more my style.

ONRAIT: Plus you're making real money now and not minimum wage.

BEADLE: [Looking me up and down] What exactly is going on here?

ONRAIT: We should go. I've taken up too much of your time.

BEADLE: That's okay. I love TSN! I love James Duthie.

ONRAIT: He's an asshole.

BEADLE: [Laughter]

And off she went to enjoy her day. What a delightful woman. I wanted to marry her on the spot. The segment was perfect. "I wish you hadn't said 'asshole,'" said our senior assignment editor, Brett Bailey, who had joined us on the shoot as a field producer.

"We'll just bleep it out and it will be even funnier!" I replied, too filled with glee to let anything get me down now. Well, almost anything . . .

We knew we probably had enough footage to put together a pretty funny little story, but we thought we might luck out and land one more star like Matt Lauer or Bruce Jenner. Imagine the reaction that former decathlete Jenner would have to seeing me in this outfit! I say "imagine" because Jenner's face is now so disfigured from various plastic surgeries that he is incapable of having any reaction to anything.

Suddenly Dave looked over at me with concern on his face. He gestured toward a group of men standing near the entranceway of the cafeteria. They appeared to have noticed us and were talking among themselves. I honestly didn't think much of it, since plenty of other people had looked at us with curiosity throughout the course of the afternoon. I was dressed in nothing but a skin-tight full-body unitard, for God's sake—we were bound to get a few weird looks.

But these guys appeared more serious. The guy in the middle who appeared to be leading the group actually looked like an athlete: tall, muscular, quite a good-looking guy actually. Was he a past Olympian working as a commentator that I didn't recognize? I was about to find out, because he and four other men were approaching us.

"Hey, guys, what's going on here?" said the athletic leader of the posse.

"Oh, hey," I replied innocently. "We're just interviewing people coming out of the cafeteria for *SportsCentre* in Canada." I really hoped that was enough of an explanation. At this point I still couldn't tell if he was just a curious passerby or someone with real power.

"What's with the outfit?" He wasn't being a total jerk, but he was a little bit condescending. His entourage was eyeing us with looks of disgust, however. They were mostly short, stocky guys— they could have all been extras on *The Sopranos*. They definitely weren't Olympic security guys, though. I still couldn't quite figure out what the hell was going on.

"I thought I'd just get dressed up a little, you know? The Games are almost over, and I didn't have a chance to wear my best outfit yet," I said to the group, half expecting uproarious laughter in return. I got nothing. Silence.

"What kind of interviews are you doing?" asked Athletic Dude, continuing to press the subject.

"Just having fun! Doing a few quick, fun interviews." I was mentioning "fun" so much I sounded like Grant Fuhr doing a postgame interview after an Edmonton Oilers game in 1987.

"Well why didn't you e-mail us? We could've arranged one-on-one interviews for you," replied Athletic Dude.

Wait . . . Athletic Dude was a public relations guy? I thought all PR people were tiny, intimidating women! Just kidding. But not really.

While I digested this information, I tried to answer his question as diplomatically as possible. He handed me his card. It read:

COMMUNICATIONS DIRECTOR, NBC SPORTS

He wasn't just a public relations guy, he was *the* public relations guy. Now, how exactly was I supposed to answer his question?

"Well, we did e-mail you actually, you and several members of your department, several different times. We've been hoping to line up some simple interviews since the start of the Games! I'm sorry it didn't work out!" It was just about as diplomatic as I could be at this point.

Suddenly the goon squad began to pipe up.

"We didn't get any e-mails like that," said one of the short, stocky dudes, who honestly looked like he belonged in a prison yard and not writing press releases for reality shows.

"I didn't get any e-mails like that either," said the pack leader. The old "I didn't get the e-mail" excuse. We've all used it at some point, and they were playing that card now. Then the stocky prison yard guy piped up again:

"You guys work for CTV, right?" Oh, crap.

Suddenly an older, angry-looking guy peered over Athletic Guy's shoulder. "I think you guys should leave," he said to us. He had an air about him that said "I am someone important, and you need to listen to what I say." He also had an air about him that said "I will die friendless and alone."

There was no point in arguing. These guys wanted us the hell out of there, so why cause a fuss? We were already in trouble with our bosses at CTV and we knew it. We packed up our gear and returned to our little office trailer in Trafalgar Square, where our makeshift studio had been set up to broadcast *SportsCentre* throughout the Games.

That evening, our piece with McEnroe and Michelle Beadle ran in the first hour of the *SportsCentre* "Olympic Suppertime Spectacular," as we had cleverly called it. The editor who put the piece together bleeped out "asshole" during the Beadle interview, and it turned out great. There's almost nothing funnier than bleeping out inappropriate words. Jon Stewart has been doing it to great effect on *The Daily Show* for years now, and Dan O'Toole and I have used it to great effect on our podcast. Despite all the crap those PR guys had given us, I was really happy with the way things had worked out that day.

Because our show was two hours, the piece was scheduled to run two times. Once we hit the commercial break, I asked our long-suffering producer, Producer Tim, if he thought I should promote the fact that the story would be running again in the second hour.

"It's not running in the second hour," he replied.

"Why not?" I wondered.

"I'll tell you later" was his explanation. Oh, crap.

Sure enough, after the show ended, Producer Tim and I talked on the phone and he explained the situation. Immediately after our confrontation with the NBC PR guys that afternoon, Athletic Guy had called CTV and told them that some "crazy *SportsCentre* guy" was harassing their talent.

My remaining segments during the Olympic shows were cancelled. No more wandering around 221B Baker Street dressed as Sherlock Holmes; no more "What the England Are You Eating?" with Dan blindfolded and trying Scotch eggs; and no more sketches featuring me dressed as a London bobby pretending to arrest tourists, even though we had already shot and edited a final one. I took some solace in the fact that there were only two days of the Games left, but I was just about ready to come home. The closing ceremony couldn't come soon enough.

That night, I got a strange e-mail from a guy in Los Angeles named Jacob Ullman, who worked for Fox Sports.

It asked, "Would you ever consider coming to work in the United States?"

CHAPTER 2

Do the Best You Can with

What You Have

I'm KIND OF AN ASSHOLE.

It's taken me a long time to come to grips with it, but it's true. I realize it's not a surprise to most of you who watch *SportsCentre*. It's pretty obvious. Even most of my heroes are assholes: Bill Murray, Chevy Chase, David Letterman, the Philly Phanatic . . . Two people did manage to keep me from turning out to be a *total* asshole, however: my parents. It's why the two-parent system works. It keeps people from becoming total assholes.

My friend Peter once described my family as "the kind that wears matching ski suits." Both of my parents were always encouraging and supportive. My mom's favourite saying was "Do the best you can with what you have." Unfortunately, she was also the first person to see my penis.

After graduating from pharmacy at the University of Saskatchewan, Dad found work behind the dispensary at a Woolco department store in Calgary in 1972. They had just purchased their first home: a modest two-storey at a relatively reasonable 17 percent interest rate. I was born two years later and apparently I was a very cute little kid. Unfortunately for my parents, I was uncomfortable with any attention whatsoever and was rather rude to anyone who tried to pay me a compliment. Turns out I was a little bit of a dickhead. Some things never change.

It was a wonderful time to be a small-town business owner, and a few years after I was born, a small drugstore came up for sale in Boyle, Alberta. My parents, my newborn sister, and I made the six-hour drive straight north from Calgary, past Edmonton about an hour and a half or so, right into the village of Boyle, population 700. Mom and Dad had both grown up in small towns, so small-town living was not foreign to them, but they had arrived on a rainy weekend. The village had only gravel roads, and the whole place resembled some sort of apocalyptic *Mad Max* scene. My mom took one look and said, "Let's turn around. We'll tell them we couldn't make it." Two days later, they bought the drugstore.

We lived in the back of the store for the first year; there was a suite back there, and that's where we all slept. My sister and I shared a bedroom, and by "bedroom" I mean the stockroom. We would spend the days wandering the aisles and reading the comics. Even today when I wander into a drugstore—with that unique smell combination of over-the-counter medicine and feminine hygiene products—I'm instantly transported back to my childhood.

In Boyle we had three channels, but the only one that came in clearly was the CBC, with shows like *The Beachcombers* and *The Wonderful World of Disney* on Sunday night and reruns of *Three's Company* and *Happy Days* airing in the afternoon after I got home from school. After the sitcoms ended, the local news began.

CBC's Edmonton newscast was anchored by a stately old codger from Ontario named Alex Moir, the quintessential old-school broadcaster like the one in the movie *Anchorman*, except unlike Ron Burgundy, you got the impression that Alex actually cracked open a few of his leather-bound books once in a while. I vividly remember Alex lamenting the state of his beloved Toronto Maple Leafs, who were an absolute laughingstock at the time. However, I wasn't too interested in Alex and the news, and I especially wasn't interested in the Leafs. I was busy obsessing over the Edmonton Oilers and their incredible young team headlined by The Great One, and during the summers, it was Gary Carter and the Montreal Expos. So the local sportscast was a massive part of my day. This was before TSN, so there were no half-hour sports highlight shows for me to obsess over yet. Little did I realize I was being spoiled with sports broadcasting talent, as CBC Edmonton unleashed a "murderer's row" of anchors who would later go on to excel on a national level.

First up was John Wells, who anchored the suppertime sportscast and hosted the western feed of *Hockey Night in Canada* as well. John was the first sportscaster I remember watching. His style wasn't flashy. He grew up in the business, the son of "Cactus Jack" Wells, longtime play-by-play man for the Winnipeg Blue Bombers. John was blessed with a voice as rich and warm as his dad's. I remember attending my uncle's wedding at age six wearing my first suit. Apparently, I told everyone at the wedding it was my "John Wells" suit. Everyone at that wedding very likely thought I was going to turn out to be some weirdo, and it turns out they were absolutely correct.

John soon moved on, perhaps the most high-profile on-air talent lured away from CBC for the launch of TSN in 1984. He was replaced by Chris Cuthbert. The same Chris Cuthbert who called the gold-medal game in men's hockey at the Vancouver Olympics and currently calls NHL and CFL games for TSN, including the Grey Cup. Before Chris got his big broadcasting break, however, he was anchoring the suppertime sportscast at CBC Edmonton, and I was watching about two feet from the TV. It was amazing whenever Chris told my co-host Dan O'Toole and me that he loved to watch our show. Not to mention the fact that he's one of the nicest people in the business.

After Chris moved on he was replaced by Gord Miller. Yes, the same Gord Miller who currently splits play-by-play duties with Chris for the *NHL on TSN* and serves as the lead voice for the World Junior Hockey Championship, one of TSN's marquee properties. Gord grew up in Edmonton, and I believe he may have joined the CBC at nineteen or something, like the Eddie Murphy of Canadian sportscasting without the leather suits (as far as I know; it *was* the '80s). He looked barely nineteen years old but his talent was obvious, and it was no surprise to see him eventually move on to TSN during the network's early days. During an e-mail exchange with Gord during the 2012 Stanley Cup playoffs, he mentioned to me that he enjoys watching Dan and me every day on his Slingbox while he's on the road calling games, and again, this was an incredibly flattering revelation for me.

After we'd been in Boyle for five years, another slightly bigger store came up for sale in the nearby town of Athabasca. I remember Dad sitting me down at the kitchen table and telling me we had bought the store and we were moving. Just as he did when Mom insisted he tell me about "the birds and the bees" because a girl in our high school had become pregnant and I was asking questions. His approach was always simple and direct: "You know those times when your penis gets stiff? It will fit *inside the vagina*."

I was excited about the move to Athabasca for one important reason: They had cable TV.

It wasn't like we were cut off from society in Boyle or anything, but suddenly a new world opened up to me. Around age twelve or thirteen I started to watch *CNN Sports Tonight* with Nick Charles and Fred Hickman, my first introduction to a big-time American sportscast. *Sports Tonight* was a simple half-hour highlight show hosted by two solid, straightforward broadcasters who wore *killer* suits. Looking back on those suits now, it was as if the two of them had raided Steve Harvey's closet: all wide lapels and bold colours and bold ties.

Sunday nights on TSN I was splitting my time between *NFL Primetime* with Chris Berman and Tom Jackson and *Trans World Sport*, a weekly show featuring sports highlights from around the globe voiced by a pleasant English woman with a posh accent. Many in my business now remember the hilarious way she would introduce NHL hockey: "Turning to North American ice hockey competition . . . "

Also airing Sunday nights on some random American channel on our cable was *The George Michael Sports Machine*, which managed to stay on the air for over two decades. George Michael (not the Wham! frontman) was a veteran sportscaster who dressed like he was christening a yacht alongside Judge Smails in *Caddyshack*. He would stand in front of a set that looked like the bridge of the *Enterprise* on the original *Star Trek* series from the '60s and ramble on about whatever highlight he was about to show you, and then he would actually reach down and push a button on his "sports machine," which was supposed to "roll the highlights" for him. This ridiculous gimmick continued for the life of the program, even after they brought on some young girl to be paired with an aging George to go after the young male demographic well after the show had run its course. There was something simple and endearing about the original *George Michael Sports Machine* to the point where I expect someone will make a movie about the show someday starring Christopher Plummer.

I was also fully addicted to NBC's hot new talk show, *Late Night with David Letterman*. I set the family's VCR on a timer to record the show every weeknight, and upon returning from school I would watch it, absolutely mesmerized. Dave was the first to "take the show out of the show" and peel back the curtain to reveal just how cheap and fun TV could be. Sending his stage manager Biff Henderson to the World Series, dropping objects off tall buildings, wearing a suit of Alka-Seltzer and stepping into a giant tub of water. Everyone I knew loved the show as much as I did. Dave was proving that television could be taken in another direction. He was acknowledging what the viewer at home was thinking in a way that had never been done before. Instead of trying to cover up his show's mistakes and shortcomings, he was deliberately pointing them out.

Soon, local Edmonton station ITV (which would eventually become Global Edmonton) launched their own half-hour nightly sports highlight show following the local late news. They called the show *Sports Night* and hired a guy named Darren Dutchyshen to host it. "Dutchy" was quick to let everyone in Edmonton know he was from Porcupine Plain, Saskatchewan, *and* of Ukrainian descent. Since half the population of Alberta at the time was from Saskatchewan and the other half was Ukrainian, he was an instant hit. Plus he had a mullet, that long, unruly, shaggy, unkempt tuft of "short-in-the-front, long-in-the-back" hair that he sported upon arrival. Similar to the long, unruly, shaggy, unkempt mullets that so many of us viewers were sporting at the time. He was one of our own.

Dutchy hit Edmonton like a rocket. He was loud, brash, outspoken, and funny, and he had just about the most unique delivery of any sportscaster I had ever seen up to that point. His personality played particularly well in blue-collar Edmonton. This was a guy you could actually imagine playing most of the pranks on your beer-league hockey team.

After a few years flying solo on *Sports Night*, Dutchy was joined by another young broadcaster named Perry Solkowski. Anyone who grew up in the late '80s and early '90s in the Edmonton area and who cared about sports has fond memories of Dutchy and Perry hosting the show together after the late news. I remember my first year at the University of Alberta. Every weeknight would end with me and my roommate Trevor flipping on ITV, watching *Sports Night*, and laughing at Dutchy and Perry. No, we were not getting laid much.

Dutchy and Perry were having an absolute blast. It was obvious just watching them.

CHAPTER 3

The Lost Years

I WAS UNSURE IF I really wanted to go on and pursue a career in broadcasting because I had heard that all Canadian broadcasters ate ramen noodles for dinner because they were so poor. Then the summer after my first year at the University of Alberta, I was working at my dad's drugstore in Athabasca and in walked Trevis Belcourt.

Trevis was a few years older than I was, and he and his younger brother Aaron were pretty unique in that they were the only guys I went to high school with who would come into my dad's store and ask if the new *GQ* magazine had arrived. While most guys in that town were reading *The Hockey News* or *Metal Edge*, Trevis and Aaron could probably have told you who Jay McInerney or Bret Easton Ellis were at the time. They were hugely into hip hop. They were not destined for life in a small agricultural town in northern Alberta.

When Trevis graduated he went straight to Toronto to attend Ryerson's radio and television arts program. He was back that summer, having just finished his final year of school, and he stopped by the store to chat. Suddenly I was captivated with stories about how much fun he had at Ryerson and how much fun Toronto was. I had already committed to attending the University of Alberta for a second year that fall, or rather, they had agreed to let me return after grades that could be described as "barely adequate." I had plans to get better grades, apply to pharmacy, and return home to take over the family business. After talking to Trevis, however, I began to ponder what it would be like if I decided to make a 180-degree turn into broadcasting.

My dad was well aware of my interest in broadcasting, and he also encouraged me to look into schools, perhaps sensing the inevitable. To that end he purchased a book called *What Color Is Your Parachute?*, a self-help bible somewhat appropriately written by a pastor, Richard Nelson Bolles. Bolles's philosophy is based on one simple fact: Everyone likes talking about themselves. The idea was to cold-call a person in the industry that you emulate, then ask for five minutes of their time over coffee. At this point said person may try to answer a few quick questions for you and then explain that they have to get back to work. Your goal is to prevent that from happening and try to get the person one-on-one. By getting the person one-on-one, you are putting a face to that cold-calling voice and hopefully establishing your first "contact" in the industry.

Bolles also suggested you speak with a professor or instructor at a post-secondary institution you think you may want to attend. No point in subjecting yourself to a terrifying cold call if you decide after speaking to someone who teaches in your chosen profession that you actually have no interest in pursuing it at all. I called the radio and television arts department at NAIT (the Northern Alberta Institute of Technology) in Edmonton. I was immediately connected with the head of the RTA program, and he graciously agreed to meet me in his office one weekday afternoon in the summer of 1993.

Much to my surprise and delight, many of my favourite local TV news personalities had gone through the NAIT RTA program, but one name stood out: Perry Solkowski. "He went here?" I said in disbelief. I don't exactly know why I was shocked, but for whatever reason it opened a mental door that had been completely closed before: *I could go to NAIT and end up working alongside Dutchy and Perry at ITV.* I was suddenly possessed of a single-minded focus to try to pursue a career in this business.

I told the NAIT professor that I was attending the University of Alberta, and he informed me that local news producer Pat Kiernan had also attended the U of A and was building a successful broadcasting career. He went on to become the mega-popular morning news host on Manhattan's NY1 news station. "My suggestion would be to get in contact with Pat," he said.

Pat agreed to meet me at Earls on Calgary Trail Southbound in Edmonton, the original Earls restaurant in fact. It happened to be right by the ITV headquarters on Allard Way, the same studio that had been home to SCTV in its third and fourth seasons. Pat was not only the producer of ITV's *News at Ten* but also the host of the *Your Money* financial segment. He was not even thirty years old. For whatever reason, Pat appreciated my initiative and told me I was welcome to come by the station any time I wanted while he was working. He said he would be able to teach me "how to write news" and that I could help out around the newsroom, but that obviously I wouldn't get paid. He had me at "how to write news," and that summer I was driving into Edmonton three nights a week, often nodding off at the wheel of my 1970 Buick Skylark on the hour-and-a-half drive back to Athabasca.

Early on during my brief tenure at ITV I was speaking to a veteran camera operator, and he was telling me about his job, the hours, and the fact that he would be working that weekend while his wife and kids were at home. He wasn't complaining because that is what he signed up for. He said, "Remember one thing about broadcasting: You will always be working when everyone else you know is off." Having someone explain the bizarre hours and lifestyle of this business before I even fully committed to it really helped me make the decision. Plus, I liked working nights; if anything, that was a bonus for me.

I spent my afternoons and evenings at the station combing the CNN television news feeds and watching *CNN Headline News*, searching for any funny and light, yet universally appealing, stories that might be good to finish off the nightly news, aka "the Kicker." I was also in charge of watching Jeannie Moos's daily report from New York, which was always quirky and hilarious. She had a unique reporting style that made her popular, covering misfits and strange characters and situations from the Big Apple. Once in a while Pat would allow me to write the copy for the Kicker. Every day that I worked, Pat and I would grab lunch with his actual NAIT broadcast intern, David Ewasuk, now a reporter at CTV Edmonton. We'd chow down on Wendy's drive-through and talk about the business. Slowly, over the course of the summer, I understood what it was like to work in the TV news biz.

All the while I was writing and learning about news, I was getting a chance to meet my heroes Dutchyshen and Solkowski in person. They were both friendly but ultimately didn't have much time for me, which was completely understandable. It was great watching Dutchy saunter around the newsroom joking happily with the news anchors and seeing Perry's casual demeanor and friendly attitude. They seemed to be having more fun than the news people.

That fall I was accepted into Ryerson, and I flew down a couple of days before my first class with a suitcase in each hand like Balki Bartokomous arriving in America from the tiny island nation of Mypos on *Perfect Strangers*. Ryerson was right in the heart of downtown Toronto, and while I didn't expect to see so many hookers on the boundaries of a university campus, I immediately felt like I belonged. I'm pretty sure all those hookers were happy for me. Welcome to Toronto, prairie boy.

CHAPTER 4

Pooping in Front of My Parents

WHEN THE HOLIDAY SEASON ARRIVES I make the cross-country flight to Kelowna, B.C., where my parents have lived since 1997. I like the joke that my mom made the decision to move to the sunny Okanagan approximately four seconds after my younger sister graduated from high school in northern Alberta. Unshackled from the brats, my folks were free to head straight to their favourite part of this great country, where they could spend their days drinking wine on the beach illegally in plastic cups. (They don't really do that.)

The Okanagan is where we and countless other Albertans spent our summer holidays when we were kids. Aside from the sunny weather, beautiful beaches, and abundant locally grown fruit, we also enjoyed the fact that we could go see movies every night. I realize that in this day and age, that makes it sound as if I grew up in a Quaker town, but Athabasca was just a small town and didn't have a movie theatre. These days we'd all just fire up movies on our iPads and ignore each other the entire vacation, but back then going to see films at the tiny, ancient four-screen cinema in downtown

Penticton, B.C., was somehow a highlight of our trip. We would show up in town and find the latest Penticton newspaper to check the movie listings for the two weeks of our vacation. Then I would carefully plan our viewing schedule. *Batman* would be first, followed by *Terminator 2: Judgment Day*, and then perhaps we would have to slum it with *Jaws: The Revenge*. It was a highly strategic planning session, and it sums up how desperate we were for entertainment at the time.

I always enjoy my time in Kelowna because I feel instantly transported to my youth, much the same way I'm sure people who grew up spending their summers in cottages and cabins and camps across the country love returning there as adults, even if it means they have to help put the dock in the lake. There's just something very special about returning to a place with so many childhood memories, a place you so looked forward to visiting in the waning weeks of the school year. Although it is true that I was forced to attend Okanagan Hockey School for one of those two weeks.

As much as I loved playing hockey, I absolutely dreaded hockey school. Having to practise twice a day wasn't so bad. I even got to meet Murray Bannerman! It was the dryland training that I really couldn't stand. Doing "wall-sits" and running the track in thirty-degree heat should have probably been tagged as a mild form of child cruelty. (I can already hear my parents laughing as they read this.) As a side note, I'd like to start a movement to have wall-sits outlawed in this country, because they truly are the closest thing to torture that I have experienced. The simple method: Find a wall. Put your back directly against that wall. Now bend your knees until you are in a "sitting" position against the wall, making sure you don't use your hands to prop yourself up in any way. "Sit" like this for as long as you possibly can without moving or falling. Personally, I'd rather be water-boarded.

If you're the kind of parent thinking about putting your son or daughter in hockey school, first sit them down and ask them this question: Does the idea of two hockey practices without shinny, followed or preceded by two one-hour sessions of dryland training, sound like how you'd like to spend your summer vacation days in thirty-degree heat? Because I'm just not convinced that these kids have any idea what they're getting into. Sorry, hockey schools across the country, the secret is out: You're running prison camps for kids, and people are paying you handsomely for it. Dictators around the world should probably fly to Canada in July and take notes.

When I land at the Kelowna International Airport these days ("Who had the balls to call it *that*?" asked comedian Jeremy Hotz upon visiting the city), I am greeted warmly by my niece and nephews, and the fun begins. My sister is two years younger than me, and like many people of her generation she loves the Food Network and food shows and has taken a liking to cooking at home. My sister really takes the reins in the kitchen around the holidays now. And what a spread she had planned for us on Christmas Eve of 2010.

When we were younger, my family would make frequent trips to Edmonton for a little family getaway. We didn't call it Edmonton, though. We called it "the City." It was the closest big city to my small town, and calling it by its name just seemed like a waste of time for everyone. It was clear which city we were talking about. We weren't talking about Des Moines.

The culinary highlight of the weekend in the City would be a trip to "Bourbon Street" at the West Edmonton Mall. Anchoring the Bourbon strip was a seafood restaurant called the Pacific Fish Company, where we would gorge on mountains and mountains of huge crab legs. As a thirteen-year-old I was pretty much convinced that crab legs were the most delicious things on the planet. All that sweet meat dipped in hot butter was a really special treat. As I got older, like many seafood lovers I began to eat less crab and more lobster, but I never forgot how delightful it was to stop by Pacific Fish for those crab legs with my parents.

My sister never forgot either. "Let's do crab legs on Christmas Eve!" she said to me with great enthusiasm over the phone weeks before I was to arrive in Kelowna.

"Sure," I replied. Gorging on seafood the night before Christmas like good Catholics and then passing out in a peaceful slumber while waiting for Santa to arrive? What could be better than that?

On Christmas Eve my parents and I made our way over to my sister's house. My sister and her husband now live in Kelowna, so the holidays are a breeze. My sister does all the cooking, or most of it. We help clean up and then retreat back to my parents' house for a peaceful Scotch or three without the grandchildren distracting us from our boozing.

As we sat down for our meal I was delighted to be transported back to my childhood. Erin had taken care of everything: a delicious salad, steamed potatoes, and of course the crab legs, which had been secured from Costco that very day. Yes, *Costco*. I once shocked my best friends by revealing to them that I thought Costco's meat department was underrated and that they should be buying steaks there. You would think I had told them to buy their steaks at a military supply store. Though I suppose at this point Costco sells military supplies as well. Those of us who love Costco are well aware that it is a great place to get steaks and seafood at great prices. That last sentence was in no way my attempt to appeal to the good people at Costco to stock this book in their stores. (At a reasonable discount, of course.)

I began cracking open those delicious crab "gams" and digging out all that tender meat inside while my dad opened the wine and my mom drank it. I am a real "dipper," so I was drowning every piece in butter. The whole experience was an absolute delight, and

I congratulated my sister on a job well done. After dessert and a bit of port as a digestif, Mom and Dad and I went home for our Scotch. We promised to return bright and early the next day to watch the kids open their presents, and my sister was already planning a massive breakfast of eggs Benedict. My sister is like Giada DeLaurentiis without the boobs!

Back at Mom and Dad's, Food Network Canada was running a marathon of one of my favourite shows: *The Best Thing I Ever Ate*. What a great show! Food Network stars describing their favourite dishes in their favourite restaurants—it's the very definition of food porn. It's also the perfect thing to watch with your parents over the holidays if the World Juniors haven't started. But around episode three, I started to realize something inside me wasn't quite right. I don't know if I had eaten too many crab legs or just caught a bug on the way to Kelowna. Whatever it was inside me that was turning my insides out, I was about to pay the price for it.

The next twenty-four hours of my life would largely consist of me expunging fluid from my anus with the consistency and liquidity of chocolate milk. First it was a violent bout of diarrhea, followed by a furious bout of vomiting, and reverse and repeat, over and over. It was completely and totally unbearable. That feeling you get when you simply can't wipe your ass anymore because it's so violently charred that it looks like charcoal in your barbeque at the end of the summer. You feel like you've been repeatedly punched in the chest because you've been heaving into the toilet for hours. As my parents quietly continued to watch *Best Thing*, I made return trip after return trip to the bathroom to relieve myself of whatever bug I had contracted that evening. Pooping and puking. Pooping and puking. Over and over and over until I was convinced I had no fluids left whatsoever and my insides must look like fruit leather.

Obviously, my parents became increasingly concerned about my condition each time I returned to join them for a brief respite in the living room. I wouldn't be back there to visit for long, just enough time to recap what was going on: "My stomach is in really, really bad shape," I said, stating the obvious, "and seeing Guy Fieri eat rib tips on TV right now is *not* helping the cause."

Right around my twentieth trip to the loo, my parents, and specifically my mom, started to become really concerned. They actually followed me to the bathroom. I had shut the door, and they could clearly hear me vomiting on the other side. "Are you okayyyyy?" asked my mom. Yeah, I'm great, Mom, I'm great. "Open the door," she said. *Why?* I wondered. "Just open it." She was not afraid of what she was about to see, but she should have been.

I opened the door.

There I was in all my thirty-six-year-old glory on the floor of the bathroom in front of the toilet. At that point I was wearing nothing but my underwear: white Calvin Klein boxer briefs (I had stripped down to almost nothing because I was sweating so badly). If that pair of underwear could talk they would have said, "Kill . . . me."

For a brief moment I thought back to what it must have been like when I was born.

It was the early '70s. My parents were baby boomers from Saskatchewan with very little money and big dreams. They were just trying to carve out a life for themselves. My dad wanted a baby boy he could send to hockey school to do wall-sits; my mom wanted a child she could nurture and raise and be proud of. It was the greatest moment of their lives! The possibilities and opportunities for their newborn son were endless.

Fast-forward thirty-six years.

There, before them on the bathroom floor, was their son sitting cross-legged in front of perhaps the most well-used toilet in North America that evening. They must have wondered, for a brief moment, if this was what it was like to have a crackhead for a son.

I stared up at my parents, who were looking down at me with faces of concern.

And I promptly shit my pants right in front of them.

Loudly.

Just imagine hearing the sound that an eight-year-old boy makes when he's *imitating* someone with uncontrollable diarrhea: using his lips and two hands to imitate a loud, flapping, wet fart noise.

Now imagine that noise, for real. I filled those Calvin Klein briefs for a good five seconds until they looked like a sausage casing trying to contain its contents. I filled my already soiled drawers in front of the two people who had brought me into this world. All the while, as this was happening, I continued to stare right into their horrified eyes like a poker player waiting for the guy across the table to make a move. The entire thing happened out of the blue and it was uncontrollable. I completely lost control of my bowels. Perhaps I was simply exhausted and could no longer control the movement of my rectum. All I know is, I was sitting on the floor in front of the toilet, with my parents looking down on me, and the next thing I knew I was crapping my pants. Loudly.

I looked up at my mom.

And I said . . . "Sorry."

"It's okay," she replied.

Have you ever taken a moment to think of all the people you could shit your pants in front of and have them simply say, "It's okay"? For most people the list is pretty short. For others the list does not exist at all. Maybe your husband or wife, but certainly not right after you've been married. Shitting your pants in front of your new spouse is pretty much grounds for divorce—they might even be able to get an annulment.

It was as if, for a moment, I had forgotten that my parents and I were human beings, and instead I was so sick that I thought we were horses.

You've seen horses take a shit while they're walking and not even break stride, right? You're walking down the street when two cops and their magnificent horses clop, clop, clop right beside you. How fun! Then one of them drops a basketball-sized turd on the road beside you. Not so fun anymore. Horses shit in front of each other *as they're eating.* I've never lived in a barn, but I imagined that shitting in front of my parents was like getting a glimpse of life as a horse in a barn. Shitting in front of the rest of the horses in my family, and then continuing on with my day.

Mom and Dad, sufficiently aware that there was nothing more they could do but pretend this entire incident had never happened, returned to watch a show about food that must have been really awful after what they had just witnessed. I continued my cycle of physical hell through most of the night, so thirsty from dehydration I would have killed someone for a carbonated beverage.

The next day Mom told me I should probably throw out the bath mat I had been sitting on that night. And the underwear. She even thought the shower curtain should be replaced. I'm pretty sure she got an entire cleaning crew in after I left to fumigate and disinfect her guest bathroom. It was likely months before she even ventured in there.

The next year we played it safe and went with turkey.

I remember when I left high school for university. Like many teenagers who grew up before the days of the Internet, I kept an entire stack of pornographic magazines hidden under my bed. When I returned home one weekend to visit, I was horrified to find out that my old bed had been replaced by a new one. "We found a deal!" said my parents. There was never any mention of the sticky, disgusting pornographic magazines that they clearly had to have disposed of. They never mentioned it once, and I was very grateful for that.

They never mention the time I shit in front of them, either, and I'm grateful for that, too.

CHAPTER 5

The First Job

MY FIRST DAY AS AN INTERN with TSN was in January of 1996. I frankly couldn't believe I was standing in the newsroom where legends of the Canadian sports broadcasting industry like Dave Hodge and Jim Van Horne plied their trade. I had beaten out a number of other broadcasting students across the country and was given a tidy $1,000 toward my education as well as a four-month work placement at Canada's Sports Leader. Needless to say I was determined to get that internship. What sealed the deal for me was my experience volunteering at ITV two years previously. It made me realize that every effort you make trying to gain experience in this business can pay off in some way.

Our current show producer, the now famous Producer Tim, and I were the only two interns brought in to the *Sportsdesk* newsroom in January of 1996, so I guess it makes perfect sense that our fates have been tied together. We worked on "the Row": a row of work pods where all the show's writers sat side by side, watching games, writing down everything that happened, and writing the highlights.

It's safe to say that probably 80 percent of the employees currently working on the television side at TSN started on the Row. It's the place where we find out if aspiring broadcasters can handle the pace of production.

I started my internship right after the holiday season sometime in early January 1996. I was twenty-one years old at the time, and I had already arrived at the place where I wanted to spend the entirety of my working life.

That's when I first encountered Mark Milliere.

When it all comes down to it, I owe my career to the man. He is a hugely successful broadcast executive and one of the most distinctive voices in the network's history. And I really mean *distinctive voice*. No one *speaks* quite like Mark. I can honestly say that everyone who works at TSN tries to do an impression of his hushed delivery at one point or another during their tenure. If I could describe it I would say imagine a combination of indifference, sarcasm, and quiet tones combined with a voice one register lower than Bubbles from *Trailer Park Boys*. I can honestly say I've never met anyone who speaks quite like him. I had several *bosses* at TSN but ultimately I answered to Mark, I negotiated my contracts with Mark, and Mark protected me from the higher-ups at CTV when they got mad at me for mentioning on air how bad I thought the show *Pan Am* was. Mark has probably saved my ass more times than he'd like to mention or remember.

Mark also had the power to fire me, and I always imagined that's how my tenure with the network would end one day. One of our online producers at TSN.ca, who would like to remain nameless, imagines Mark would get a kick out of firing people using knock-knock jokes:

"Hey, Jay," he would come up to me and say.

"Yes, Mark?" I would reply.

"Knock knock."

"Who's there?"

"You're fired."

Something succinct like that. Mark is a man of few words.

These days Mark's title is executive vice-president of production, and he is basically in charge of the entire on-air look of the network and all the shows, but when I started back in 1996 Mark was one of several producers on *Sportsdesk*. He produced the 6:30 edition of the show, which was hosted by Jim Van Horne at the time. I met him on my first day at the network, or should I say, I was *ignored* by him on my first day at the network.

Wearing what was probably a T-shirt that featured a box of Trix on it or maybe the Brillo logo, I tentatively approached Mark, who was sitting at his regular desk in the middle of the newsroom typing away on the computer.

Gwen, the newsroom assistant, had already told me to ask Mark what my first task would be. Also known as "the first day of the rest of my life" (cue the *Perfect Strangers* theme).

"Hi, Mark!" I said cheerfully. "My name is Jay. I'm the new intern from Ryerson. Anything I can help you with to get started?" I was pretty good at introductions, even then.

Silence.

Not just silence, but a complete lack of acknowledgement. Mark was completely ignoring me. Not saying "Just hold on a sec, I'll be right with you" or "Hey, man, come back in five minutes."

It was literally as if I weren't standing there at all. I might as well have been invisible.

Jim Van Horne was sitting in the desk next to Mark typing away as well. I looked over to him for something, anything, but he didn't look up, either, nor did the person sitting on the other side of Mark.

It was as if I were in one of those movies where I die and then come back as a ghost, and I'm trying to get people to pay attention to me for several scenes. Later, I finally realize I'm dead and that I have to help my former fiancée meet a new man and move on with her life, or something like that. You know the film. It stars me and Ricky Gervais and Whoopi Goldberg and probably features a dog as the only character in the film that can see or hear me.

Finally, after what seemed like five minutes of standing next to this man looking like a complete idiot, I sheepishly wandered back to the Row, where all the show's writers sat and watched games. Given that it was an afternoon in the middle of winter, there were likely no live sports to watch, so I chatted away with everyone else, including Tim, not yet Producer Tim, still an intern like me. Tim had arrived earlier than me and had also been stonewalled by Mark, which made me feel slightly better but still very confused. Is it possible that I might be ignored by this guy for the entirety of my four-month internship? Was it my responsibility to hit him across the head to get his attention? My head was filled with anxiety when I was suddenly awakened from my daydream by a very distinct voice.

"Jay!" said Mark in about the loudest voice level I've heard from him before or since.

I spun around. He was talking to me! *He was talking to me!*

"Right here!" I said, just a *touch* overenthusiastically.

"Where the hell have you been? You were supposed to start fifteen minutes ago."

Was this a joke? Was someone playing a joke on the new guy? I stared at Mark, who had the stone-faced expression of an angry parent. No, this was clearly not a joke.

"I've . . . I've been here the entire time. I came up to say hi to you fifteen minutes ago. Do you remember?"

Mark not only didn't remember he didn't care. "I need you to watch ABC news feeds for anything we might want to use in our "News and Notes" segment. Can you do that?" he asked.

I had watched news feeds while volunteering at ITV, so this was actually a job skill I had already acquired: watching TV. Truthfully, I had been preparing for this job my entire life.

"No problem, Mark."

He turned away again.

That would be all I would see or hear from Mark for the next three hours, right up until 6:00.

At that time we were still recording our stories, highlights, and features on Beta tape. This may seem archaic, but Beta was the format of choice for years in broadcast news because of the quality of the picture. So instead of having all the video exist on a hard drive as it does today, we would have multiple tapes for each show. By the time 6:00 p.m. rolled around, we were a half-hour to showtime. In a normal newsroom all the tapes that would be used in that show would mostly be gone, either already handed in to master control for playback or in use by one of our editors, perhaps putting the finishing touches on our lead item. Mark worked a bit differently.

I started to notice that every single day, right around 6:00, *almost all* of the tapes would still be sitting on a table near Mark's desk, waiting to be assigned. This was different from other editions of *Sportsdesk* that I would work on, where the tapes would be assigned much earlier, like at the beginning of our shift, so we knew what we were actually supposed to be doing. Mark's was the only show where a half-hour before we were scheduled to go live across the country most of the items in the show had not been assigned yet and a large stack of tapes sat next to his desk, unclaimed. I wondered about this but decided it was above my pay grade (my pay being nothing), and therefore I shouldn't worry about it. I began to realize that Mark thrived on chaos. When the clock struck six, it was as if an alarm bell went off in Mark's head. Suddenly, he would jump out of his chair and begin to assign stories and items in the show to people in a seemingly random fashion, throwing the Beta tapes at us like footballs. It was never boring. The shows were always great and every tape made it to air. It was his way of operating, and it worked for him.

Now he's in charge of TSN's network content, and that's working out pretty well for him, too. Unfortunately for Mark, he was also in charge of my show. But fortunately for me and Dan, he always supported it. The fact that I worked for him all those years ago as an intern and then as a story editor convinced him to trust me when, years later, I would come up with ideas like having one of our own writers get slapped by Dan on live television. I never fully appreciated all the freedom Mark gave me to be creative until I went to work for someone else. You need to have someone who has your back in this business, and Mark always did.

CHAPTER 6

We Are All Nerds

IT WASN'T LONG AFTER I joined TSN as a writer back in 1996 that I started to realize that professional wrestling wasn't dead.

In the popular culture of the day, pro wrestling was indeed dead, about as uncool as an entertainment genre could be at the time. The stars of the '80s, like Hulk Hogan and the Iron Sheik, were getting older, and those of us who had grown up in wrestling's incredible nadir surrounding the first three WrestleManias had now also gotten older. Too old to continue watching men throw each other around in a ring and brandish their considerable freestyle skills on the microphone. For me at the time, the concept of watching wrestling was as ridiculous as the concept of playing with the Star Wars action figures I had collected as a kid. Sure, I would have enjoyed the tugging on my heartstrings of nostalgia for a moment, but ultimately, I was a grown-up, and watching wrestling was supposed to be for kids.

How naïve I was.

Soon after being brought into the network as an intern I met

Steve Argintaru, who rose through the ranks to the position he holds as of this writing: executive producer of *SportsCentre*. Steve is a smart, hard-working guy and a talented broadcaster, but it became very clear to me very quickly that as much as he loved professional sports, his true passion was professional wrestling.

Steve was a few years older than me and seemed like a nice and normal guy, so imagine my shock when he told me that in his spare time he was a freelance photographer for *Pro Wrestling Illustrated*, a trade magazine that peaked in popularity during the '80s by ranking the wrestlers and tag teams of the era in top-ten formats, regardless of organizational affiliation. I was under the impression that *Pro Wrestling Illustrated* had probably folded years ago, but that wasn't the case. In fact, Steve wasn't the only wrestling fan in the *Sportsdesk* newsroom; it turned out that the people in the newsroom were a great example of a sports nerd microculture, and that to many of them wrestling was still a fun way to kill an hour or two on a weekend.

Soon after I arrived at TSN, wrestling experienced a comeback with the likes of The Rock and Stone Cold Steve Austin leading the way, and I'm sure Steve felt vindicated for sticking with his beloved men in tights, as he should have. It was the first time I began to really feel at home in a television newsroom, a place where nerds thrive and jocks can sometimes feel left out. The newsroom is almost the opposite of a pro sports dressing room: Suddenly no one cares about their prowess on the ice or the court. They're more curious whether anybody watched the previous Sunday's episode of *Game of Thrones* after catching that double overtime between the Hawks and Celtics.

I met more nerds in the TSN *Sportsdesk* newsroom in the early '90s, but these nerds were not interested in wrestling—they were too high-minded for that. These nerds were into music. They were into music as much as they were into sports! They were just like me!

In fact, they were better nerds than me. Way better. Now at work on *Sportsdesk* in between innings of my Cubs–Cardinals afternoon game, I suddenly found myself chatting with my fellow writers about whether Len would be more than just a one-hit wonder (they weren't; it didn't take a nerd to figure that out).

$$\lightning$$

One of the reasons I enjoy the writing of Chuck Klosterman so much is that I feel like we have such similar backgrounds. Chuck grew up in rural North Dakota, loved hair metal bands growing up (he even wrote a book about them called *Fargo Rock City*), and most importantly, he actually played sports in high school like I did. There was a simple reason why Chuck played sports and didn't just watch them like most nerds. When you grow up in a small town there are fewer kids competing to be on the local sports teams, and you get opportunities that city kids might not get. That was certainly the case for me, though I was also lucky to be tall and semi-athletic (notice I said "semi-athletic"), so I was able to play hockey and volleyball and even basketball, a sport I loved to watch but didn't love to play. When you are over six-foot-five in a town of fewer than 2,000 people, there is a very good chance you will be playing on the high school basketball team. I'm glad there wasn't a football team for me to try out for. I would have likely ended up with some sort of severe injury.

If you're familiar with Klosterman's work you know he is almost as comfortable writing about sports as he is about music and pop culture. Sports and music pretty comfortably fall under the banner of pop culture these days because they're all about entertainment, and if you're even younger than Chuck and me, then you are probably even more comfortable combining every-thing under that banner because all your information, music, and possibly even television and movies are coming from one place: the Internet. It's safe to say that Klosterman could be classified as a nerd. He looks like a nerd. He certainly *sounds* like a nerd. And he writes with nerd-like obsession about subjects he is passion-ate about. That's my message to you aspiring sports broadcasters and journalists out there: Embrace your nerd-dom. The best way to prepare yourself to stay employed through the ever-changing ways we deliver information to the public is to *be* a nerd: some-one who is so vastly knowledgeable about a subject that he or she transcends all the mediums it might be delivered through. The medium is no longer the message, the message is the message! Suck it, Marshall McLuhan.

So when I arrive at a newsroom for work, the first subject of conversation will likely be the games we are watching on the mon-itors. Some guys might talk about fantasy pools they're currently in; others might talk about sports news they heard about that day that is now seven hours old, practically ancient history by modern media standards. Then talk inevitably moves to television and which shows we're watching, because every single person in that newsroom isn't just a sports television nerd, they're a television nerd, *period*. Shows like *The Wire* and *Game of Thrones* are held in particularly high regard because, being as obsessive as we are about the medium, we seek out only the very best from it. Not to mention the fact that once one group in the newsroom starts watching a show you can't fall behind, because that group will inevitably want to discuss said show at work the next day, and there's an excellent chance those shows will be spoiled for you if you haven't watched them.

Then there's movie talk: Producer Tim is a particularly big fan of discussing the latest Hollywood blockbusters. He is a moderate Michael Bay apologist, which is still completely unacceptable to me to this day. Finally, talk often drifts to music with certain people in the room, the music nerds. The sports nerds who unwind after a day of watching three baseball games by putting My Morning Jacket's *It Still Moves* on their Bose Wave music player while they finish off the last beer of the day. I tend to gravitate toward these nerds in the newsroom, and they tend to be the people I attend concerts with, just as they are also likely the people I would attend an afternoon Blue Jays game with. Nerds are nerds are nerds. The people running the Canadian television sports networks are some of the biggest nerds in the world. I should know, because I work for them, and they speak my language.

So if you're the kind of person who thinks you might want to become a sports broadcaster, here's a tip: Lock yourself in your room with your TV or iPad or computer and about six or seven great sports books about subjects that interest you, and just start devouring knowledge like an ancient Greek philosopher. Jump on YouTube and check out clips of games you've heard about but never seen. Watch as much sports as you possibly can without alienating friends and family. Heck, invite your friends and family over to watch sports. Don't forget to make nachos. Every single day, read every single sports writer whom you respect and admire, and even some of the ones you don't admire. And maybe even start a blog and a Twitter account and start writing yourself.

I still maintain that the ability to write well is the single most important tool that will help you succeed in this business. In the past you didn't have many outlets to allow you to practise writing in a professional style. Now with every great sports writer published online, you can follow your favourites and try to develop your own style, maybe even get some feedback along the way. The next generation of sports broadcasters and journalists will be much more informed than we were, thanks to the wealth of knowledge available to them, literally, at their fingertips. By the way, you realize what I'm saying here, right? I'm telling you that the way to succeed in my business is to just watch sports. That's it. Could anything be more simple and awesome than that?

CHAPTER 7

The Man Who Hates When Things Happen

I MENTIONED THE OTHER INTERN brought in that semester in 1996 was the man who would eventually be known as Producer Tim. He wouldn't be given this nickname until years later, when he became a regular producer for Dan O'Toole and me on *SportsCentre*. The question I get asked most wherever I go is "Is Producer Tim real?" The answer is yes, he is absolutely a real person. I think because you never actually see him, people assume we've made him up as some sort of character on our show. He's definitely a character, but he's also definitely not make-believe. Tim is a human—the most stressed-out human who ever lived on the planet Earth.

It was Dan who started to mention Producer Tim on TV during the actual show, and that's because Dan and Tim have a hilarious, contentious relationship that Tim accuses me of facilitating with my devious ways. Tim is a full-on stress case. Even when Tim and I started as interns at the network in the same week, I quickly came to the realization that Tim was not a man who took things lightly. As much as I try to pretend otherwise, I am pretty much exactly the same way, and that's probably one of the many reasons why Tim and I have always, for the most part, gotten along well.

Tim is a *planner*. He is a man who puts his show lineup together nice and early and gets extremely stressed out when he has to change it. This is not a good trait for a television producer in terms of stress, because a TV news show's lineup will change several times a night. It's *news*. You can't really plan it. You have to adapt on the fly. Tim would prefer that the news adapt around *him*. Dan has a pretty good nickname for him: The Man Who Hates When Things Happen. It will probably be the title of Tim's tell-all book when he decides to expose us for the high-maintenance "poodles" we are someday.

When Dan started to mention Producer Tim on the show, I was initially a little apprehensive. *Is this a little too inside?* I wondered. It was supposed to be a sports news show after all. But we had already blurred the line from a strictly *sports* show to a *sports show with heavy dollops of absurdity*, and there was no turning back now. Especially since Mark Milliere seemed to love the idea instantly. Maybe it was because Mark himself had been a show producer, and he appreciated the idea of Tim becoming a recurring "character" on the program. Mark is also the kind of person who seems to have a particular fondness for people who have the potential to publicly freak out about things. I think it amuses him.

Four months after Tim and I started at the network back in 1996, I learned first-hand that one mistake on the Row can end your career at TSN almost immediately.

I was working one Friday night, and we were leading off our show with Toronto Argonauts highlights. Much to my chagrin, a fellow intern who had just been brought in was given the assignment of watching the game and writing the highlight script. (We'll call him "Mike" to protect his identity, and also because about 50 percent of TSN male employees are named Mike anyway.) Trying to contain my jealousy that I hadn't been given the top story, I continued to work on what was likely an Atlanta Hawks–New Jersey Nets barnburner at the old Omni in Georgia. Hours later I looked up at one of our in-house monitors and noticed the show was starting. I had already pretty much finished my script and was just kicking back, enjoying the final, inconsequential seconds of the Hawks game, when I noticed that something was amiss . . .

One of the show's anchors that night, Brendan Connor, seemed to be stalling for a long time. A *very long* time. Keep in mind that in television a long time is thirty seconds. Thirty seconds in the real world is not a long time. Thirty seconds in television is an eternity, and it was *very* clear that something was amiss with Mr. Connor. I wondered what was happening since I knew Mike had been assigned to that lead highlight package. He happened to be sitting two pods next to me, so I wandered over.

"Hey, Mike," I said.

"Hey," he said.

"Did you put together the Argos pack?" I asked.

"Yeah, it's done. What's the problem?"

I looked down at his desk, and there was the tape that the pack had been recorded on. Mike had forgotten to actually give the tape to our master control operator so they could, you know, play it during the show. He looked up at me in horror.

"FUCK ME!" he screamed, sprinting into the master control room, waving the tape. "FUCK ME!"

But by then it was too late. Brendan had run out of things to say about the Toronto Argonauts, and the show's producer made the decision to show a scoreboard of the game in progress and then move on to another highlight package. Mike's internship ended then and there.

While Mike didn't survive that summer, I somehow managed to stay on as a freelance story editor while attending Ryerson. My days back then were an absolute dream. I would take a half-hour subway ride, then a half-hour bus ride to the studio. I loved the solitude of public transit, and this was even before the days when iPhones were there to entertain you. I would arrive at TSN and be assigned a couple of games to watch and write highlights for. My sports knowledge was not even close to the level of most of my colleagues, but it improved immensely just by virtue of the fact that I was watching so many games. And did I mention I was *watching television and getting paid for it*? I honestly couldn't believe it. I was also writing highlights for *Sportsdesk*'s new anchor team, Darren Dutchyshen, my hero, and Mike Toth.

I actually ended up really bonding with Mike. Mostly, he was just weird and made me laugh, and I've always loved weird people who make me laugh. He once told me that while hosting prime-time highlight shows on TSN and Sportsnet, he would often write the show in an hour, then leave the newsroom and head to a nearby theatre to catch a movie, returning just in time to host his live show. His reasoning: "They're paying me to do the show; they're not paying me to get *ready* for the show."

Years later when I was trying to decide whether or not to leave *The Big Breakfast* in Winnipeg and join the NHL Network I asked Mike for advice, and he recommended that I not take the job. His main reason: the NHL Network was a digital cable network at a time when not many people had digital cable. Why make the move to sit in front of so few eyeballs? When I eventually took the job anyway and ended up appearing nightly on TSN at midnight to host *That's Hockey 2*, Mike called me and said, "Good thing you didn't take my advice!"

CHAPTER 8

I'll Pull Your Cable Anytime

AFTER A YEAR AT TSN, when I had successfully established a place for myself at the network, I started to inquire about the possibility of following our local Toronto reporters around to gain some experience in the field. Between full-time school and almost full-time work (I was pulling about four shifts a week), it wasn't easy to find time to do this. Especially since I had no money, no car, and basically no brains. Luckily, the Toronto Maple Leafs were still playing at Maple Leaf Gardens, and the Gardens was only a two-block walk from my place at Ryerson. Rod Smith, Lisa Bowes, and Susan Rogers were our regular Toronto reporters at the time. Ask any veteran TSN cameraman who the best reporter in the history of the network is and they will almost always have Rod at or near the top of the list. He was not only born with a voice that would be appropriate for that of God in a stage adaptation of *The Ten Commandments*, but he is an outstanding journalist and writer as well. Rod is also an exceptionally kind-hearted man, and he never cringed, at least outwardly, when I'd show up at the Gardens for Leafs practice and ask if I could "pull cable" for him.

I realize that if you've never worked in the television broadcasting industry, the term "pulling cable" may sound like slang for gay sex. I can assure you that no gay sex occurred between Rod and me—though, let's be honest, I would have done *anything* for a chance at an on-air gig. Pulling cable is really just keeping a hold on the cables that the camera and microphone might be attached to so no one trips and dies. In the case of field journalism, a cable puller is rarely required because the camera is powered by a battery, but that didn't stop me from pretending my presence at Leafs practices was necessary.

I'd show up at the Gardens wearing one of two blazers I had purchased from International Clothiers. Both jackets had been purchased for a total of $99 and were made of fabric that could best be described as "likely flammable." After pulling cable for Rod or Lisa while they gathered story clips from players and shot their own stand-up for the story (the part of the story when the reporter literally stands up and talks into the camera, usually at the end), Rod would then hand the microphone over to me and allow me to basically say what he had just said. Albeit wearing a much, much cheaper jacket.

The first couple of times were terrifying, and like all rookie reporters I would make the mistake of memorizing what I was going to say instead of simply making sure I knew my key talking points and trying to articulate them. Still, after a few trips to the Gardens and the SkyDome with Rod, I started to get more comfortable.

I had ordered a horribly written book by two aspiring sports broadcasters titled, appropriately, *How to Make It in Sports Broadcasting*. I say it was a "book," but it was really about as thick as a leaflet when it arrived at my door at 182 Mutual Street in Toronto sometime in the fall of 1997. But I did take one important aspect from the "book," which I likely finished during one prolonged bowel movement: In the television broadcasting industry, a person's demo tape should be no longer than five minutes, the first minute consisting of a montage of fifteen-second stand-ups and desk reads, ideally two of each to get to the minute mark. The opening montage served to remind everyone that television was, in the end, a visual medium. No sense in presenting your brilliant two-minute story right off the top if the news director you were applying to didn't like the way you looked. The opening montage allowed news directors to see what you looked like on camera and hear your voice; if they liked what they saw or heard, then they could continue to watch and see if you were a good storyteller. If they didn't like the way you looked or sounded, no amount of storytelling brilliance was going to get you that job.

So I continued to try to get my "reps" in following Rod and Lisa and Susan around town. I remember once I was sent, alone, to Maple Leaf Gardens to interview then Leafs-owner Steve Stavro about the hiring of Ken Dryden as new Leafs president. In addition to being one of the greatest goaltenders to have ever played in the National Hockey League, Mr. Dryden has a reputation for being a *tinge* long-winded when he speaks in public. This day would be no exception. As Mr. Dryden went on and on about "completing his career" by "helping the Maple Leafs win the Stanley Cup," I thought about writing a commercial spoof for *Saturday Night Live* called the "Ken Dryden Sleep Inducer," which would simply have been a small playback machine with a speaker that spoke to you in Ken's dulcet tones until you were lulled into a peaceful slumber. Listening to Ken Dryden speak in public is a little like listening to Ben Stein in *Ferris Bueller's Day Off*.

When Mr. Dryden had finished speaking and answering questions, a scrum of reporters gathered around Mr. Stavro to ask him about the hiring of Ken Dryden. I was first up. Or rather, I blurted my question out like an idiot before anyone with real credentials would get a chance to do so. And I began my question by addressing the Leafs owner and multi-millionaire at the top of my lungs:

"STEVE . . . " I started.

My camera operator, Tim Moses, a veteran of thousands and thousands of sports shoots, tapped me on the shoulder and in front of the entire Toronto media at the time corrected me:

"MISSSSTER Stavro."

I was humiliated. *What a douche I am*, I thought. I recovered quickly and likely asked him how soon he expected to break their Stanley Cup jinx. Two years? Three years? Surely it wouldn't take more than five. This was 1996.

Meanwhile, back in the newsroom I was still working as an editorial assistant. I was kept on at the network throughout my final two school years at Ryerson. I would work nights, usually until midnight or 2:00 a.m., and then return home to an old rat-infested house I shared with my college roommates near the corner of Jarvis and Gerrard in downtown Toronto. Those of you familiar with Toronto may know the corner of Jarvis and Gerrard as the location of "Hooker Harvey's," a Harvey's restaurant frequented by the ladies who walked the nearby streets of what was then Toronto's thriving red-light district. Many a night I would return home from work at TSN, get off the subway, and be greeted on Carlton Street by a steady line of leather- and latex-clad prostitutes, who started to recognize me and couldn't have been sweeter even though they were plainly aware I didn't have the cash to spend an hour in their company.

I'd get home and settle on the front porch with one of my roommates, drinking a few beers. You could see the back of Hooker Harvey's from that porch, and we would laugh as we watched the hookers give out hand jobs behind the restaurant. This was the real definition of "pulling cable." Guys would pull their jeans halfway down their legs, and the prostitutes would half-heartedly yank away like they were playing the slots in Vegas. If I had a nickel for every time I saw a guy get an awkward standing hand job from a lady of the night, I'd be a rich man by now. It was like having the world's worst live sex show performed just for you every night. Life was pretty good!

In addition to allowing me to record fake stand-ups for my demo tape, TSN was also gracious enough to let me bribe one of our editors with booze to help me put together a couple of actual stories for my demo. This merely involved taking a story that Rod or Lisa had already done, rewriting it in my own, less eloquent words, and tacking my stand-up on the end. Same clips, different voice, different reporter. The stories weren't spectacular but the camera work was wonderful, and boy, did it look great to see me holding a TSN microphone. I still needed to do some desk work, however.

I was terrified the first time I did a demo on the actual desk at *Sportsdesk*. Dennis Beram is currently the most senior show producer at TSN and the person who knows more about sports than anyone I know. He was producing all the "*Sportsdesk* Updates" that night, the one-minute sports package that would run at the top of every hour and still does on TSN to this day. I approached Dennis about stepping behind the desk and simply doing the exact same update Brendan Connor would have just done. The crew all reluctantly agreed to let me do it, just as all television crews reluctantly agree to work with me to this day.

Once again, I grabbed one of my International Clothiers jackets, and with my palms sweaty and my brain running a million miles an hour, I waited as the *Sportsdesk* crew set up in the control room and made sure one of my co-workers was available to run the teleprompter. Thank God it took only one take. I made it through an all-important Milwaukee Brewers highlight package, smiled at the end, and signed off. After it was over Dennis came up to me and said, "That was pretty good!" It wasn't an encouraging, nurturing "pretty good" like my mom would have given me. It was an "I can't believe that was pretty good 'pretty good.'" Coming from someone like Dennis, who held all sports anchors to very high standards, it was the greatest compliment I could have received. I ended up doing a couple more demos on the desk, and suddenly with my stand-ups, fake stories, and one-minute updates I had plenty of material to put together a respectable demo tape. The question was: Would there be a job for me when it was all done?

CHAPTER 9

I Wear the Pants

AFTER TWO YEARS OF WORK at TSN and following the completion of my degree at Ryerson, I, like a lot of kids my age, backpacked through Europe with my best friend. Although backpacking was the experience of a lifetime, three months of wearing the same pants is not something I would recommend. I literally wore the same pair of beige corduroys for ninety straight days, washing them perhaps three times. Looking back, I can't believe I was wondering why I wasn't getting more action. I did manage to make it to Wimbledon for a glorious day of tennis before returning home completely broke. Beyond broke, actually. I had to borrow funds from my parents just to make it home. Upon my arrival back in North America, I burned the pants. I'm surprised they didn't start themselves on fire as I walked around Europe with those dirty fibres rubbing together.

Back in Canada, I suddenly had no job and no place to live, so I travelled across the country by car to visit my parents at their new home of Kelowna, B.C., where they had chosen to retire. Instead of going straight to Kelowna I thought I would fly to Regina, visit my grandfather, and then rent a car and travel west, visiting every single TV station along the way. I was hoping to meet a ton of news directors and drum up some interest in me. I concentrated my search in western Canada because I knew the terrain, and the cities and stations were very familiar to me. After a couple of days of driving and meeting and greeting, I came upon Lethbridge, Alberta, fourth-largest city in Wild Rose Country. Following a quick visit at the Global TV station in town, I made my way to the CTV station and was greeted not by the news director but the nighttime news producer, who couldn't have been nicer about a total stranger and gangly idiot interrupting her workday. She told me the same thing everyone along the trip had told me: NO jobs to be had at her station.

But she did offer me hope . . .

She mentioned that six months previously, her main sports anchor had left Lethbridge to take a similar job at Global Television in Saskatoon. However, his fiancée had stayed behind in Lethbridge. The sportscaster was not happy being away from his lady love and had been making noise about wanting to return home. The nighttime news producer surmised that there would therefore be a job open at Global Saskatoon within a few weeks, and if I was smart I would contact the news director there. I never got the name of that nighttime news producer, but I wish I had. She essentially jump-started my career without knowing it.

The next day I was on the phone to Global Saskatoon and their longtime news director Lisa Ford, who had earned the nickname "Lita Ford" because, well, she basically looked the way you would have imagined the former member of the Runaways would look like twenty years after "Kiss Me Deadly." I mean that in the best way possible. Leather jackets, long blonde hair, boots. She was awesome. I chatted with her over the phone briefly, and she told me to send her my demo tape and she would get back to me.

I went to visit my parents for a week, during which time I was in constant contact with Lisa. I don't know if I have ever been more determined to land a job in my entire life. The entire situation was perfect. Saskatoon was a city I'd been to many times before. There was a major junior hockey team (the Blades), and the University of Saskatchewan had some of the best athletic programs in the country. The junior football team had an especially storied reputation, and the city actually rallied around them and the other U of S sports programs. What *really* made the job special was the fact that they were still producing a local *Sportsline* highlight show right after the late news. Instead of having little more than four or five minutes to fill during the local newscast, I would be responsible for co-hosting and helping to produce a half-hour nightly highlight show. The perfect training ground for a future TSN anchor. Not getting this job would be devastating.

I returned to Toronto, where I still had no place to live. Luckily the house right behind Hooker Harvey's where I'd lived my last two years at Ryerson was still occupied by my best friends from school, and there was plenty of room and plenty of old, disgusting couches in the basement for me to crash on. TSN had generously agreed to bring me back on as a freelance editorial assistant. I could easily have picked up my life right where it had left off, late-night hand job shows and all, but I was now obsessed with landing that job in Saskatoon and getting my on-air career started.

Two weeks later I got the call. Lisa wanted to hire me as the new sports director at Global Saskatoon. As it turned out, not only was one of her sportscasters returning to Lethbridge, another one was leaving to take a job at CTV in Ottawa. That meant there were two jobs to be filled, including the person who would be in charge of the department. In the wake of Sportsnet launching that fall and *The Score* having been on the air for a couple years, Lisa had been experiencing frequent turnover in the sports department, as more and more anchors had been treating Saskatoon as a pit stop on the way to bigger and better things. I didn't have the heart to tell her that I planned to treat Saskatoon as a pit stop on the way to bigger and better things. She hoped that by handing me a job that was over my head I would grow into it and, more importantly, stick around for a little while. Like for five years. I had no problem with this idea. I had two weeks to pack up the few clothes I had, book a flight, and start my new job.

CHAPTER 10

I'm on TV!

I WAS HAPPY TO HAVE LANDED my first real on-air broadcasting job in a city of 200,000 people and not 20,000 people. Instead of me finding an apartment in Saskatoon right away, my parents arranged for me to rent a room with my great-uncle Reg, whom I had visited once in Florida but never really spent much time with. In hindsight it was like the set-up for an '80s sitcom or a Bravo reality show: Young hotshot sportscaster moves in with seventy-year-old retired model plane enthusiast and hilarity ensues. Like a multi-generational *The Odd Couple*.

Uncle Reg was a widower who had a nice bungalow about a ten-minute drive from the TV station. I had my own room and my own bathroom for the bargain price of about $300 a month. I was more than happy to stay with him, and we hit it off right away. Reg was long retired from working at General Motors, and when he wasn't working on model airplanes in his basement and terrorizing the waitresses at the local Zellers diner, he was probably having a nice long nap. He was also a natural-born jokester, and I think he genuinely enjoyed having the company after having been alone for at least a decade at that point. His wife, my auntie Joyce, had died relatively young. He had a large mirror hanging in his entrance-way, and I used to love to pretend to fix my hair for about ten minutes before I left for work every day, much to his disgust. He would retaliate by draping a towel over said mirror for me to witness when I arrived home. Just a couple of frat boys we were.

About a month into my job, my new co-anchor on *Sportsline* at Global Saskatoon, Derek Bidwell, told me he was having a Halloween party and invited me along.

Derek was a classic life-of-the-party guy, the one in the middle of the room good-naturedly making fun of everyone and making them laugh. He was born and raised in Saskatoon and had played for the Hilltops Junior Football Team. It seemed like the entire town showed up for the party at the bungalow near downtown that he was renting with a couple of his buddies. Derek dressed as a wizard or something and wore this long robe—it was a little like something you'd imagine Hugh Hefner wearing at the Halloween party at the Playboy Mansion. The party was a blast until everyone in the living room heard a massively loud THUMP and looked down the stairs into the basement to see Derek sprawled on the floor in significant pain. He was attempting to head downstairs to get more beer when he tripped over his flowing robes and went tumbling down to a likely concussion. He was off work for several days. I'm pretty sure he's recovered, though with Derek it's sometimes hard to tell. He will enjoy that joke.

I had brought along my favourite booze mix from university: beers and tequila. Back at Ryerson it was my drink combo of choice. I genuinely always loved the taste of tequila even before we all started drinking *good* tequila. For Derek's party I thought I'd bring tequila for everyone and get the party going, but the party was already going when I got there, and for some strange reason no one was that interested in drinking the tequila except me. I had even brought along salt and limes in a little Ziploc bag. It was all a little "Anal Retentive Fisherman" of me. It goes without saying that I had way more than my share of tequila that night.

I remember taking a cab home, and as the driver pulled up to Uncle Reg's mid-century bungalow, I puked all over the backseat. I am still amazed that I remembered the address in that state. The cabbie was obviously furious. I threw one twenty at him for the cab ride and another for his trouble, and by "his trouble" I mean my vomit. Somehow I managed to stumble into the front door. Once inside I tried desperately not to wake Uncle Reg, who was scheduled to begin the drive to his winter home in Florida the next day on November 1, the same trip he made every year. Once I had started vomiting beer and tequila, my stomach was not about to stop until all the offensive residue had been purged from my body. I puked violently and loudly throughout the night, relieved that I did indeed have my own bathroom and was not sharing one with Uncle Reg. My great-uncle was a sound sleeper, and I peeked in on him a few times to make sure I hadn't awakened him with my juvenile antics. I finally got to sleep around 4:00 or so.

The next day I was scheduled to host *Sportsline* at 11:00 p.m. For the average hangover it's reasonable to assume that by 11:00 p.m. you should be somewhat recovered and perhaps ready to go out and accomplish whatever task is in front of you, but on this particular day the booze had hit me harder than usual. After dragging myself into the shower and throwing on a suit, I went into the TV station and spent a good portion of the day sleeping on the couch in Lisa Ford's office. I felt like absolute death, and it wasn't getting any better as show time approached. To this day, I have never been that hungover in my entire life. Somehow I managed to finish writing all my scripts and even edit my own highlights, but this was interrupted by frequent trips to the washroom to vomit and to wish death upon myself.

I made a promise: If I was able to make it through that broadcast, I would never, ever drink heavily the night before a broadcast again, no matter how late the broadcast was the next day. Clearly a recovery time of more than twelve hours was still not enough for my delicate body.

As 11:00 p.m. drew closer I began to have serious fears: My nausea had not subsided, and I was going to be sitting on a desk for half an hour with no chance for a quick bathroom break. The commercial breaks were only two minutes long, and the bathroom was a one-minute walk from the set. It began to dawn on me: Exactly one month into my broadcasting career, there was a very good chance I was going to vomit uncontrollably on live television, thus ending my career in one of the most spectacular flame-outs in the history of the business. I was destined to become an urban legend. All of this also occurred just as the Internet era was about to blossom, meaning there was a good chance that someone would save the tapes of the incident and I would become one of the first YouTube sensations. My chances of career recovery would be slim.

I emptied a garbage can under my desk in the newsroom and brought it up on set with me. At the very least I could lean down and puke into a bucket like a normal person rather than doing it all over the desk like some neanderthal. That would show class and sophistication on my part. Maybe that would save my job: "Jay, we're really disappointed that you puked on live television; *however*, nice work bringing the bucket up to the desk! Quick thinking!"

I sat down in my chair behind the *Sportsline* desk and organized my papers. Once the opening theme music kicked in, my mind started to focus and my stomach started to feel better. Somehow I made it through the show that night. A little adrenaline kicked in and settled my stomach just enough to get me by. I drove home, relieved that I wouldn't have to head in early the next day to face my boss and explain myself for the vomit—that someone now had to clean up off her set—just before I was escorted out of the building.

As for the promise I made to myself to not drink that heavily the night before a broadcast ever again, I have kept it, for the most part. I was never very good at leaving the party early, and someday it will probably be my downfall.

Six months after the near-vomiting experience on the set of *Sportsline*, I had moved out of the bungalow and was now living in my own apartment in downtown Saskatoon. Uncle Reg had just returned from Florida, and I drove up to his place for dinner and a visit. It was nice to see him, hang out for a bit, and hear his stories about all the older ladies who had been "pawing at him" throughout his time in Florida. When he was ready to crash I got up to leave. I made sure that he saw me stop and check my hair in the mirror in the entranceway, and then I started out the door. Uncle Reg waited atop the front steps as I walked toward my car, and just as I was about to open the driver door he called out, "Oh, by the way, I hope you got someone in to clean the bathroom after that night before I left."

I looked up and saw him smiling.

"You were on the big white telephone with Ralph all night!"

CHAPTER 11

Pinball Was My Bieber

AFTER MY INITIAL BRUSH with death by vomiting in my first
month on the job, I started to settle in at Global Television. At the
ripe ol' age of twenty-four I was hosting *Sportsline* five nights a
week at 11:00 as well as a short four-minute segment on the 6:00
news. I was also in charge of assigning stories to the other two guys
in the apartment. Derek worked alongside me during the week. The
weekend anchor desk was manned by R.J. Broadhead, who was just
making the transition from radio to television at the time. I thought
R.J. was an excellent broadcaster, and we got along swimmingly.
His voice was so powerful it was almost like he was putting it on,
but then you met him in person and realized that he had just been
blessed with an incredible set of pipes. His father was a longtime
Saskatoon radio host, so R.J. came by his talents honestly. I'll always
remember that after Lisa told us she had hired him, Derek mentioned that R.J. had left a message on the sports department phone.
He said he couldn't believe the voice. He played it for me, and I
sincerely thought R.J. was doing a bad impression of Troy McLure

from *The Simpsons*. It was like the imitation I do of a "broadcaster," all overexaggerated syllables and dulcet tones.

Derek recovered from his brush with death at Halloween and remains a friend to this day. Having made the move to Calgary years ago, he has worked steadily in radio and television there ever since. Whenever I talk to Derek these days about our time working together in Saskatoon, one of the things I love to bring up with him is the Big Bang Incident.

This had nothing to do with the popular CTV/CBS sitcom of the same name, which was not around at that point—a good thing for me because I probably wouldn't have been secure enough at the time to accept everyone telling me how much I look like the guy who plays Sheldon on that show, actor Jim Parsons. Since I joined Twitter I probably hear that I look like Sheldon ten times a week, and it's not necessarily intended to be flattering. Nonetheless, this particular Big Bang Incident involved something different entirely.

It was about two months after I had started at Global Saskatoon and one month after the worst hangover of my life. My new boss, Lisa Ford, called Derek and me into her office and informed us we would be emceeing a Champions for Christ luncheon that was set to take place that week, and it had all been arranged by a salesperson at the station. Derek accepted this without question, but I was taken aback. "A *Champions for Christ* lunch?" I repeated with massive skepticism. "Is it even appropriate for us to be involved with that?"

It was and remains to this day a completely legitimate question. Champions for Christ is an organization that brings pro athletes of Christian faith together under one roof to do charity work and celebrate the teachings of Jesus. I knew they did a lot of wonderful work in helping those less fortunate. I also knew I did not share their beliefs, and I felt that was reason enough for me to not have to participate in this luncheon. Take my beliefs away and I still found it inappropriate for us, as the news-gathering arm of a television station, to align ourselves with Champions for Christ. It was one thing to sell ads to them promoting their luncheon. They had every right to promote whatever they wanted as long as they were willing to pay for the advertising and weren't offending anyone. However, to have anchors from the station emcee their luncheon was inappropriate to me. Just as inappropriate as having one of the station's news anchors emcee a political fundraiser.

Lisa did not understand my concern. What was the big deal, she thought? You show up, introduce the guest speakers, eat a free lunch, and leave. Derek just didn't care. He was friends with the salesman whose Christian beliefs had led to CFC advertising on our station, and he was the one who wanted Derek and me to emcee the event. If we were to drop out, Lisa would need to find someone else, which would be a headache she didn't want to have to deal with at this point. Had I flat-out refused on the basis that I didn't share the same Christian beliefs, then I obviously wouldn't have been fired, but I knew I would be labelled as a guy who wasn't a "team player." Even my new friend Chris Krieger, the station's news anchor and obviously a good judge of what was and wasn't appropriate in our business, thought I was being too much of a stickler about the whole thing. "In the end it doesn't really matter that much," he said.

So, a few days later, Derek and I made our way to the luncheon along with our camera guy, Paul Yausie, who was going to get some footage of the event to send to Champions for Christ later. Everyone attending could not have been nicer. I decided to just relax and go with it. Admittedly, I was also somewhat excited to hear the guest speaker that day: Mike "Pinball" Clemons.

Pinball was a running back for the Toronto Argonauts of the Canadian Football League and had put together a prolific Hall of Fame career. But that's not why the man is such a beloved figure in the Canadian media landscape. He's a beloved figure because he is one of the most charming and charismatic athletes to play pro sports in North America over the past three decades. He speaks passionately, smiles constantly, and has an incredibly infectious way about him. For years people have asked Pinball when he is going to run for public office, maybe even mayor, but so far he has resisted that calling. He coached the Argonauts on two separate occasions, but after his playing career he generally made his living as a motivational speaker.

After we briefly introduced ourselves, and then a man of the cloth said grace, the entire group dug in to the catered lunch. We happened to be sitting at the same table as Pinball, and he was gracious and kind to everyone seated around him, asking and remembering names, essentially interacting with people like a really good politician would. I told him I wasn't really a fan of him in his playing days because he had repeatedly burned my Edmonton Eskimos. This delighted him to no end. Unlike a politician, from Pinball you got the impression the laughter was genuine.

After lunch was over it was time to introduce Pinball. He approached the stage to high fives from the crowd and gave Derek and me a big hug as we passed him the microphone. He then completely took over the room, speaking like a southern Baptist minister. A more gifted orator you would likely not find anywhere. He talked about his personal belief in Jesus Christ and how Christ's teachings had made him a better player and person. The content of the speech wasn't groundbreaking; he was literally preaching to the choir. The delivery was mesmerizing nonetheless. I was riveted by Pinball's ability to capture the attention of the audience, moving from one side of the stage to the other, making eye contact with everyone in the room. A true professional speaker and worth every penny.

Then Pinball made the decision to attack those of us skeptical about Bible scripture, those of us who believe that "science" and "evolution" are the primary reasons that life exists on this planet today. In particular, Pinball wanted to discuss the now widely accepted big bang theory, which states that the universe essentially exploded into creation millions of years ago, leading to evolutionary life on planet Earth. We may have learned about it in high school science class, but even if Pinball had been paying attention in those classes he was having none of it. As far as Pinball was concerned, the story of Adam and Eve was the only logical explanation for life on Earth.

"Are you telling me"—now Pinball was *really* getting fired up— "that millions of years ago, there was a big bang? And after this so-called big bang, POOF! There was Derek . . . "

Pinball gestured to Derek, and Derek looked over at me. Suddenly, out of nowhere, we had become a part of the show! Even though I thought a large part of what the man on stage was saying was complete gibberish, I would be lying if I told you I wasn't waiting in giddy anticipation for Pinball to mention me too.

"Are you also telling me . . . "

Here we go . . .

"That millions of years ago, there was a big bang, and POOF! There came Jay?"

Pinball gestured to me. Pinball mentioned me! You could not wipe the smile off my face! This must be what it's like when teenage girls are pulled onstage at a Justin Bieber concert. Pinball was my Bieber!

I didn't leave the luncheon a religious convert, and I still thought it was inappropriate that we were asked to attend and emcee the event, but the truth is, in the end the entire exercise was pretty harmless. I learned one important thing that day: Pick your battles in this business. Sometimes being known as a "team player" is better than fighting for principles you don't really care too much about anyway. It's not a defeatist attitude, it's a practical one. Sometimes you just have to say "Poof" and let it slide.

CHAPTER 12

Goin' to Winnipeg. . .

AS MUCH AS PEOPLE MIGHT THINK I am some sort of pop culture junkie, I don't watch entertainment shows like *etalk* or *Entertainment Tonight*. This is not a comment on the abilities and attributes of the fine people working on those shows. I just don't like the presentation style that has become ubiquitous with them. SHOUTING LOUDLY AND BOLDLY while posing in some sort of weird cross-legged stance so I can understand just how important this upcoming story about John Travolta's latest masseuse is. It's just not me. It's just not anyone, really. If someone actually came up to you on the street and started talking to you like that, you would think they were a bloody lunatic. Whoever invented this presentation style should be exiled from the industry and forced to work with mannequins. I'm pretty certain that would be preferable to them anyway.

I have hostile feelings toward these types of shows because it was their resurgence in the early part of this century that ushered in the death of the half-hour local sports highlight show where I got my start. All across the country, Global Television had *Sportsline* shows that provided a half-hour of daily highlights and local sports content you couldn't really get anywhere else. The greatest thing about these shows was that they provided the ultimate training ground for any aspiring sports broadcaster. Those shows were never ratings blockbusters, more like niche cultural mini-blockbusters for local sports fans. So it wasn't entirely surprising that Global scrapped all their *Sportsline*-style shows across the country and replaced that half-hour of Canadian content with *Entertainment Tonight Canada*. Despite my mixed feelings, I had always been a bit curious about the world of entertainment television. I wondered if I could fit into it with my own presentation style. That is to say, with no style at all.

I started to think about applying for entertainment reporter jobs. This was still pretty much pre-Internet, when even a small start-up local TV station had two full-time entertainment reporters! You had four media outlets to inform you of entertainment happenings in your city: radio, TV, newspapers, and of course the local alt-weekly left-leaning newspaper, which probably had the best local entertainment coverage of all of them.

Around this time, Manitoba-based Craig Media was launching another one of their not-so-successful A-Channel stations in Winnipeg. Ads were plastered on the back of *Playback* magazine, an industry paper, announcing openings for on-air and behind-the-scenes talent for this exciting new start-up station, which in this case wasn't really a true start-up because the Craig family were just rebranding their already existing Manitoba station to match their two television stations in Alberta.

At no point in my life had I ever imagined moving to Winnipeg. I didn't have any preconceived notions about the city, I just never really thought about it unless the Jets or the Blue Bombers were playing. Still I thought I'd send a demo tape to the station anyway.

I didn't think I'd be contacted about a job, but maybe I could get a bit of feedback about whether going in the entertainment direction was even a viable option for a complete and utter jackass like me.

I sent a VHS tape (still prominent in 1999) to A-Channel news director Darcy Modin, and she called back surprisingly fast. Shockingly fast, actually. I should have realized I was immediately in a position of bargaining power, but I was simply too surprised by getting a phone call at all. Darcy told me the entertainment anchor posts had been filled, and she was actually wondering if I might be interested in hosting the station's brand new morning show, *The Big Breakfast*. Years later Darcy would reveal that her first two choices for the job had fallen through over, surprise, money. Turns out A-Channel was a bit desperate. Desperation! The gateway to opportunity! (That was an alternative title for this book.)

While travelling in England in the summer of 1998 I had seen the U.K.'s version of *The Big Breakfast* on Channel 4 with Johnny Vaughan and Denise Van Outen, and it seemed like a laugh riot and something I'd love to try. Darcy offered to send me a few VHS tapes of Calgary's *Big Breakfast* show starring Dave Kelly and Jebb Fink so I could watch them and have an idea of what I might be getting myself into. They arrived a couple of days later, and I popped them into the VCR at my apartment near the legendary Bessborough Hotel in downtown Saskatoon. I was immediately captivated by the show. Dave Kelly was the absolute perfect morning show host, like a young Regis Philbin. Perky, friendly, good-looking, but not *too* good-looking, the guy positively radiated energy, but not in an *annoying* way. The guests and subjects he tackled were actually interesting to me. Local restaurant chefs, local bands, and local entertainment happenings. To sum up, the whole thing was very *local*.

The thing I liked best of all was the free-flowing nature of the show and the sense that the hosts were genuinely enjoying them-selves. While *Sportsline* had been a very structured and classic-style nightly highlight show featuring teleprompter reading, highlight reading, and a bit of occasional banter, *The Big Breakfast* was pretty much the exact opposite: three hours of pure mayhem on the prairies. No script, no prompter, no rules! The formula was relatively simple: One main host in the studio, another co-host on remote, and a news anchor, preferably female, who bantered frequently with the main studio host and kept the show a little bit grounded. It was, for all intents and purposes, a note-for-note rip-off of Citytv's *Breakfast Television* format that had been so successful in Toronto. Without all that pesky traffic and transit reporting getting in the way of the fun.

Darcy liked the demo tape I had sent her for the entertainment reporter job but wanted to see something more. "Could you head out onto the street in Saskatoon and interview people and ask them interesting questions?" Um, no, I'm pretty sure me stealing a camera for an afternoon would arouse the suspicions of my current boss in Saskatchewan, I replied.

"Well, I need to see something more than just you reading highlights. I need to know you have the personality to pull this off." I should point out that at the time I wasn't exactly dressing as the Phantom of the Opera and screaming at the viewer every five minutes like I did on *SportsCentre*. Other than dressing up in an afro wig and disco outfit for Halloween I had kept things pretty normal at *Sportsline* (admittedly, dressing in an afro wig might not be considered "pretty normal"). The demo tapes I was sending out reflected a young, competent, but fairly boring broadcaster. Not much "personality" to be seen there. Luckily, I have friends who are a lot more talented than I am.

My friend Jeff Cole was in my class at Ryerson and is now a highly sought-after freelance television director and cameraman in Toronto. He was the guy at Ryerson that *everyone* wanted to have working on their projects, because he was the guy at Ryerson who actually knew what he was doing. One day in 1997 I told him I was going to try my hand at stand-up comedy at Toronto's Laugh Resort alongside my much funnier friend Peter Sayn-Wittgenstein. The Laugh Resort was located in an old firehall on Lombard Street. The one-time home of Second City in Toronto, the club would hold an amateur night every week. Peter and I, longtime fans of stand-up comedy, thought we'd give it a shot.

We had just returned from a weekend trip to New York where we had hit up the legendary comedy club Catch a Rising Star. The headliner that evening happened to be a young comedy writer named Louis CK, who at the time was just beginning his stand-up career. I'll never forget how Peter and I sat in the front row and literally laughed until we cried at Louis's incredible set, despite the fact that the rest of the crowd pretty much sat in stone-cold silence. I vowed to follow his career from then on, hoping he might catch a break and make it big someday.

I made two appearances at the Laugh Resort in Toronto, and my best joke involved an article I had recently read in *Details* magazine (back when people read *Details* magazine, or should I say, back when people read magazines at all) about how gender roles were reversed in the porn industry: The women had all the power and made all the money, while the men made next to nothing and had to wait around all day to get called to the set, leading luminaries of the genre like Peter North and Randy West (why were so many male porn stars named after directions?) to complain that they had "no life."

"So let me get this straight . . ." I said onstage in my best stand-up delivery, "they sit around all day and do nothing, and then get called to a porn set to have sex with beautiful women and get paid for it? No life? *That's my ideal life!*"

Needless to say, my stand-up career was short lived.

Thankfully, though, Jeff Cole kindly attended one of my few

appearances and, as he always did, brought his highly sophisticated VHS camera along to record the proceedings. Afterward he gave me the tape, and I sent it home to my mom for safekeeping.

Fast-forward years later and I'm on the phone with Darcy talking about the *Big Breakfast* job, and she's asking me if I have "anything else that might show my personality."

"Well, a couple of years ago I did some amateur-night stand-up comedy, and I may have a tape of it floating around somewhere."

"I need that tape," said Darcy, in the same ultra-serious tone she would use to say "I do" during our wedding four years later.

Soon I was off the phone with Darcy and on the phone with my mom in Kelowna, asking her if she wouldn't mind digging through their basement and tracking down a VHS tape that said "Jay's Stand-Up" on it. Luckily, I am the light of my mother's life, and she managed to find the tape in question almost immediately, shipping it off to Winnipeg later that day. Two days later I got a call from Darcy asking if I would like to be the new host of Winnipeg's only local morning show.

I was a steadfast negotiator. I flat-out refused to accept anything less than $48,000 for my first year and $53,000 my second year after initially being offered $40,000 for year one and $45,000 for year two. Read all about my negotiating tactics in my next book, *Zero Leverage: The World of Canadian Television.*

Truthfully, it was a big salary bump from what I was making at the time, and at this point it wasn't really about the money anyway. It was time to try something different and challenge myself a bit. I had been given the sports director job in Saskatoon based on the promise that I would stick around for five years, but it was time to move on and Lisa wasn't too upset about it. She said some wonderful things to me when I told her I was leaving, telling me I had really grown as a broadcaster and she was sad to see me go. I really appreciated how kind she was. I was sad to be leaving Saskatoon for other reasons. I had made amazing friends there in a very short time, people I remain friends with to this day. I will never forget my time in that city, but it was time to start wandering back east.

Goin' to Winnipeg . . .

CHAPTER 13

Felching Is Funny

MY CO-HOST ON *THE BIG BREAKFAST* was Jon Ljungberg, a Massachusetts-raised stand-up comedian by trade who, when travelling through Winnipeg twelve years earlier, met a girl at a gig. The next thing you know, he had two kids and a nice bungalow in the Windsor Park area of town. We immediately hit it off. I remember walking into the station for the first time and seeing him in a Hawaiian shirt, like a complete parody of a stand-up comedian. He was so friendly and immediately offered to take me "for a drive." I assumed at that point I'd either get fed or raped, and I thought it was probably pretty likely the former. Off we went, and within twenty minutes we were having a conversation about how funny the concept of "felching" was. Felching is a sex act in which a man extracts his own semen out of his partner's anus through a straw. Literally in tears laughing as Jon waxed poetic about the concept, I said to myself, "I will get along with this person. This person and I will be friends." We are still friends to this day. And felching is still hilarious.

We would have about eight thirty-second "chats" on the show every single morning, five times a week for two years. Jon's sense of humour, like mine, was mostly just silliness. We would tape "best of" shows at places like the amusement park and the Forks Market, stopping at various businesses and using props or eating food. I knew everyone in the city within three months. The mayor, all the restaurant owners, all the local bands, they all came by to be on the show. It was really fun. I would have loved to have been making more money, but I didn't think about it that much.

When I finally met Darcy in person I was swept off my feet. She was so sexy and so indifferent to my antics, but she was a good boss who gave Jon and me a lot of leeway to have fun and be ourselves. I was really starting to show my personality on television—three hours of unscripted live TV will do that for you. The only catch was working mornings, something I did not handle well back then and still don't to this day. Jon asked some of the local radio DJs for advice about how to feel more awake while doing the show, and they all said, "You will never feel awake while doing a morning show." It was a bit like the advice the camera guy gave me at ITV: *You will always be working when everyone else is off.*

I told Jon I had a crush on our boss, and he laughed at me and wished me luck. During the first A-Channel Christmas party in December 1999 I decided I would approach her about going on a date. I figured that everyone at the party had been drinking, and if she was appalled or offended or worse wanted me fired, I could explain it away the following Monday morning by telling her I had had too much to drink and didn't mean what I had said.

We were living together within a year.

I really had no plans to leave Winnipeg. I honestly thought I might never leave.

CHAPTER 14

Humiliated by a Woman on Live TV

"Ever been in a bar fight?" asked Boston Celtics star Kevin Garnett to TNT NBA reporter Craig Sager after a particularly contentious win over the Orlando Magic in early 2012.

I've had my ass kicked in a bar once or twice. Most recently, it happened just before I left my first wife. Our relationship had truly hit the skids, and I was out with Dan O'Toole and a few of his friends one night. I'm not a person who has ever enjoyed nightclubs very much, but they insisted on hitting a typical douchified Toronto establishment, the name of which I will withhold to protect the innocent. Having had a few too many cocktails, I was susceptible to engaging in conversation with people I shouldn't have, and when a beautiful blonde woman recognized me from the show I couldn't help but lap it up a bit. I was feeling lonely and miserable and fully aware I was probably about to get divorced. The lovely blonde and I made our way upstairs to continue our conversation in private in the VIP room.

After what was probably a half-hour of serious flirting, and perhaps even some light petting, I suggested we take the party to a nearby hotel. While the blonde was trying to figure out how to reject my offer as painlessly as possible, I was suddenly attacked out of nowhere. I didn't even get a good look at the guy, but the next thing I knew I was being punched square in the forehead four times. Fortunately for me, my forehead is a massive target. Any other part of my face would have been much more susceptible to real damage. A bouncer rushed over to pull the guy off of me but it was too late. The dude had been wearing a ring and cut me wide open. I started bleeding everywhere. While the guy screamed and yelled at me while being bear-hugged by a King Kong Bundy look-alike, I glanced over at the blonde, who gave me a sheepish "I'm sorry" look. Jealous ex-boyfriend. I should have known. I guess that was karma for the whole "attempting to cheat while you are married" thing. Not my best night out on the town in Toronto but a lesson learned: You should always be prepared for something bad to happen.

A couple of years before that I got my ass kicked even worse. And here's the rub: It happened on live television, and the person who kicked my ass was a very, very powerful woman. In both cases I was not prepared for what was about to happen. In both cases I suppose you could say I got what I deserved.

If people regularly watched me host *The Big Breakfast* in Winnipeg, the first thing they ask me about is the time I was beaten up by Dominique Bosshart. Dominique had just won a bronze medal in kickboxing at the 2000 Summer Games in Sydney and had returned home to a hero's welcome, fielding plenty of national and local interviews about her success. Eventually, she was kind enough to show up on *The Big Breakfast* one morning to not only answer a few questions about her time at the Games but also do a quick demo with me on kickboxing technique.

We liked to "do things" on the show, and what could be more fun than a powerful, athletic woman showing off her greatest kicks? We planned it out before the segment started: Dominique and I would talk for a minute or so about her experience in Sydney and what it's like to return home an Olympic bronze medallist, and then she and I would stand face to face and she would demonstrate a roundhouse kick, with me holding up a thick pad about waist-high to protect myself. No head gear, no other padding, just me and my Backstreet Boys outfit and my heavily gelled frosty tips to protect me. What could possibly go wrong?

Before the segment started, Dominique showed me how to hold up the protective pad, and by "protective pad" I mean a rather thin gym mat you would expect children to do somersaults on in kindergarten. For some reason this seemed perfectly reasonable protection to me. Did I mention before that I'm not much of a details guy? Dominique and her coach, who had joined her that morning, wanted me to hold the protective pad up high, so that the bottom was around belt-level and the top was just around my chin. But I was having none of it—I had visions of her perhaps losing her footing and kicking a bit lower than normal, with her foot ending up promptly wedged into my balls. Instead I insisted on holding that pad just a *little* bit lower to protect myself in the nether regions. After a few practice kicks during the commercial break, in which Dominique gave about 22 percent effort, we figured we were ready to go. We had to be ready to go . . . we were *live.*

The plan, which, yes, seems flawed now but at the time seemed brilliant, was to have Dominique go *all out* with her roundhouse kick like she would in a competition. *All out.* Again, this seemed like a perfectly reasonable plan to me. No one ever accused me of being smart. The segment started off beautifully: She was a seasoned pro and had given a million interviews, so she was friendly and comfortable on camera. Once I saw the "3 minutes left" sign from my floor director, Chris Albi, we were off.

"Let's demonstrate a roundhouse kick," I said with the confidence of a much smarter man. For whatever reason, instead of standing in a ready position with one leg firmly planted behind the other and knees bent like I was about to start a race, I decided the better option was to stand straight up with my feet right next to each other. It was as if I thought I was waiting in line for Tragically Hip tickets. Any reasonably strong human could have walked by me in that stance and shoved me over onto the floor.

"I'm ready!" I said with a smile.

They might as well have been my last words.

Dominique and I stood face to face as planned, and suddenly I had this feeling of terror wash over me. She exhibited the stance of a real kickboxing champion, and I quickly realized I may have made a horrible, horrible mistake. Too late to turn back now, however, as we were *live*. Live television doesn't wait for the man who finally realizes he's about to be humiliated in front of his audience.

Her coach counted her down: 3 ... 2 ... 1 ...

With the speed of a young Ben Johnson, his blood filled with illicit substances, Dominique spun around. Next came her powerful, powerful leg, swinging toward me like I was a piñata. Her foot hit me square in the protective pad, and I felt like I was an extra on *Bloodsport* and had just taken one straight in the gut from a young Jean-Claude Van Damme. But it wasn't just the kick. It was the momentum of her pure power that simply overwhelmed my very slight frame. This was not going to end well ...

The woman had so much power, and I was so very weak and barely awake, that I was sent barrelling backward ten feet, stumbling and trying to maintain my footing along the way. There was no stopping it. In hindsight, I should have tried to fall to the ground, but in the split second it happened there was simply no way to change my momentum. I was heading straight backward, and the only thing that was going to stop me was a big brick wall. Attached to that big brick wall? A beautiful, expensive, and somewhat brand new neon sign that lit up and said *The Big Breakfast*.

I was heading straight for that sign.

Purely by instinct, I reached out for the wall as I was falling into it, putting my hand straight into the sign and smashing it upon impact. That was followed by my entire body colliding with the sign, smashing it further and rendering it relatively unrecognizable. The bulb was destroyed, the massive neon coffee mug was destroyed, and "Big" and "Breakfast" were destroyed. Only "The" remained from an otherwise horrible mess.

After I had completed mass destruction (all of this taking place within about five seconds), I fell to the ground in a heap on top of a couple of amplifiers that had been set up for that morning's musical guest. It took about one and a half seconds for everyone in the crew, everyone in the newsroom (which faced our studio and offered a beautiful view of the entire incident), and everyone who was a guest on the show to digest what they had just seen. That was followed a half-second later by all of them bursting into uncontrollable laughter. They had just witnessed the ultimate live TV moment: a morning show host getting his ass kicked by a woman and destroying property in the process. Again, I'm amazed this clip hasn't ended up on YouTube somewhere, and I imagine that someday it will.

I slowly made my way to my feet as floor director Chris Albi showed the only concern for my well-being. You could hardly blame everyone else for standing back and enjoying my humiliation. It was hilarious and clearly my life wasn't in danger—only my pride and my gut were in pain. The real victim was that neon sign. It was destroyed beyond repair and had to be replaced. Dominique wasn't too concerned. She had known what was going to happen. The segment appeared on every "best of" show we ever did after that, and eventually they replaced that sign.

CHAPTER 15

What Do You Mean, They're Not Going to Call Them "the Jets"?

I WAS ABLE TO RETURN to Winnipeg in early April of 2012 for the Winnipeg Jets' final regular season game in their first year back in Manitoba's capital. When I lived in Winnipeg in the late nineties and early aughts, there was never any speculation about the team's returning, because no one thought it was even remotely possible. They were gone, and they were gone for good. My favourite local Winnipeg band, jazz/hip hop/instrumental collective, the Hummers, even called one of their albums *Save the Jets* in 2001 as a joke about being late to the party to keep the team in Winnipeg. I never got the feeling the city was still devastated about the loss of the team when I lived there, because enough time had passed and I think Winnipeggers had fully come to grips with it. It was only when NHL Southern-belt teams like the Atlanta Thrashers and, yes, the former Jets-now-Phoenix Coyotes began to struggle that suddenly there was a glimmer of hope.

The city had built the 15,000-seat MTS Centre for their American Hockey League team, the Manitoba Moose, as well as for concerts, and it was a tremendous success, but there was a perception that the rink was simply too small to lure an NHL team back north of the border. There was also a perception, and I fully believe this was held by NHL senior executives like Gary Bettman, that the city was simply too small and obscure a market in this day and age to house a pro team in one of the four major sports.

Luckily, a guy who happens to be the richest man in the entire country and one of the twenty richest men in the entire world thought otherwise. When David Thomson saw the way principal owner Mark Chipman was handling the day-to-day business of running the Manitoba Moose of the AHL, he soon bought out all the other partners until it was only Chipman and Thomson writing the cheques. Thomson's family had donated the land the MTS Centre sat on downtown, and he clearly saw the potential of an NHL return in the city.

⚡

Meanwhile, during the summer of 2010, Dan and I hosted a live *SportsCentre* show as part of the Kraft Celebration Tour in Pinawa, Manitoba, about two and a half hours east of Winnipeg. The show was marred by heavy rain, which didn't dampen the spirit of the incredible crowd that showed up (sorry, sometimes I can't help but write like a guy who has worked in television news for almost twenty years). We noticed a couple of people wearing Jets jerseys and asked that they be moved up closer to the stage. Then we decided to jump into the crowd while everyone chanted "BRING BACK THE JETS!" as the credits rolled. It was one of the more memorable show closings we've done, and it reminded me of the passion that Manitoba sports fans had for their team. Turns out I was just scratching the surface of that passion.

Toward the end of the following NHL season, the word had gotten out that the Atlanta Thrashers were in serious financial trouble and that a move to Winnipeg was imminent. By now it was impossible for Gary Bettman to prevent one of his prized Sunbelt teams from heading back north, even if he did show up at the press conference announcing the purchase of the team with a scowl on his face that made him look like a petulant child. "This doesn't work if the building isn't full," he sneered to Jets fans. Jets fans promptly sold out the entire 2011–2012 season in thirty minutes. There was money in the Jets ownership; the fans had proven their lust for NHL hockey by purchasing tickets in droves; and the building was in place, even if it was small by NHL standards. The Jets were back.

But would they be called "the Jets"?

Amazingly, before the deal was finalized to move the Thrashers to Winnipeg, rumblings throughout the hockey world began to occur indicating that Mr. Chipman might not want to call the team "the Jets" for various reasons: Having built up the "Moose" brand over the past few years in the Winnipeg market, there was some speculation that True North wanted to retain that moniker for the new team. There was also speculation that the owners were concerned that if the team was called "the Jets" and they wore the old uniforms, no one would buy team merchandise—probably the single dumbest argument I've ever heard. I'm pretty sure that after fifteen years of the team being away, people needed to buy themselves new Jets jerseys because of weight gain and potential lingering odour issues. There was also talk of a "fresh start" and that the "Jets" name had technically left with the old franchise that was now in Phoenix. It was genuinely thought that the new NHL team in Winnipeg would be called something other than "the Jets," and that was simply not acceptable to me.

The tradition of the "Jets" name goes back to the days when the team was a member of the World Hockey Association in the '70s. The city's long aviation history of both aerospace development and housing a Canadian Air Force base was the reason for the name, and it had a great ring to it. When the Jets moved from the WHA to the NHL they kept the name, just as the Edmonton Oilers, Quebec Nordiques, and Hartford Whalers had done.

The team enjoyed some great years throughout the '80s and early '90s with players like Dale Hawerchuk, Teppo Numminen, and Teemu Selanne. Unfortunately, the Jets never competed for a Stanley Cup because they were stuck in the Smythe Division with the all-powerful Oilers and Flames teams of the '80s. When I thought about pro hockey in Winnipeg, I immediately thought "Jets." To consider calling them something different was turning one's back on the history of hockey in the city. There were some in Winnipeg who thought a nice compromise might be to call the new team "Winnipeg Falcons" after the senior men's amateur team that won the first-ever Olympic gold medal for men's hockey back in 1920. It still made little sense to me.

Had Mr. Chipman and Mr. Thomson simply declared at the press conference announcing the purchase of the Thrashers that the new team would be called "the Jets," the entire city would have been thrilled and never even speculated about an alternative. Instead they said that a name had not been decided. There was talk that like the AHL team, they wanted "Manitoba" in the title and not "Winnipeg." I was seriously concerned. It was great that NHL hockey was returning to Manitoba's capital where it belonged, but the idea of that team not being given the name "Jets" was strangely upsetting to me. Even though I had never been a Winnipeg fan growing up, it simply *didn't seem right.*

Jay Onrait

When the city of Cleveland lost the Browns in 1996, the city negotiated a deal with the NFL to retain the Browns' name, colours, awards, and archives for three years until a new stadium could be built and the NFL would return to the city. When the city of Seattle lost the SuperSonics in 2008, civic officials also negotiated to retain the Sonics' name and colours for when the NBA returned to the Pacific Northwest. The concept of calling these teams anything else was patently absurd to all their fans.

The thought of having the NHL return to Winnipeg without them being called "the Jets" so infuriated me that I went on *SportsCentre* one day and indicated to Dan that if True North did not refer to the team as "the Jets," then I would, in fact, "lose it." I still get asked to this day what exactly that would have meant. I'm still not sure. It's not as if I was going to hop on a flight to Manitoba and try to find Mark Chipman so I could beat him up or something. He *did* grant every Manitoba hockey fan's greatest wish by returning the city to the NHL, after all. Let's just say I would have been very, very disappointed and would have very likely referred to the team as "the Jets" on *SportsCentre* even if they were called "the Falcons" or something else. Much as I often refer to the Minnesota Wild as "the North Stars" when reading their highlights.

In the end, the fan base made sure their voices were heard, and even though I'm not convinced he was completely happy about it, Mr. Chipman relented to popular opinion. When taking the microphone to announce the selection of Mark Scheifele in their first NHL draft since returning to the city, Mr. Chipman announced the pick on behalf of "the Winnipeg Jets" as several Jets fans in Jets gear who had driven down to St. Paul from Manitoba for the draft cheered in delight. I don't think my thinly veiled threats on national television tipped the scales or anything. Oh, let's be honest, of course they did. You're welcome, Winnipeg. You got your Jets back.

$\boldsymbol{\displaystyle \frac{}{}}$

After the Jets' return had been set in stone for the fall of 2011, Dan and I once again hosted a live *SportsCentre* show in Manitoba, this time about an hour west of the city, in MacGregor. The new Jets logo had already been revealed and merchandise was flying off the shelves. We expected a few new Jets caps in the crowd of about 1,000 people, but we were not fully prepared for the rowdiness of said crowd. They were nuts, and they were nuts about their newly reborn NHL team.

Bryan Little, who had played in Atlanta and was set to become one of the Jets' top forwards that fall, had agreed to come up to MacGregor and sign autographs for people in the crowd. The line to get his autograph was ridiculously long, snaking around the stage. Sean Thompson, one of our lighting guys on the Kraft Tour who looks identical to Nickelback singer Chad Kroeger and played him in sketches on our show, was placed next to Bryan and was also signing autographs. What a bizarre little world we had created. We then brought Bryan onstage so he could soak up the atmosphere a little bit. At various points during that afternoon as the crowd chanted "BRY-AN LIT-TLE," I saw Bryan, a very shy guy, glance over at us with a look that said "What the heck have I gotten myself into?"

It wasn't until the end of their first season back that I made it to a Jets game in Winnipeg. By then I had witnessed the incredible crowd on television. Everyone was blown away by the reception they gave Teemu Selanne when he returned with the Anaheim Ducks; the team's home record was substantially better than their road one; and they were at a disadvantage on the road, having to play in the Southeast Division and travel regularly to Florida and

Carolina. By season's end the Jets had fallen just short of their play-off goal, but I was still excited to finally see a game in person at the MTS Centre. I caught a last-minute flight with my girlfriend, and we checked into the Fairmont and made our way down Portage Avenue to the Jets' new home. We were escorted to the press box and had the chance to sit next to our TSN Winnipeg bureau chief, Sara Orlesky, who was a born-and-raised Winnipeg girl and had been delighted with the opportunity to work in Winnipeg full time and return to the city to raise her young daughter.

Needless to say, I was absolutely blown away by the passion of the crowd. Before the puck even dropped the team handed out several year-end awards. The reception Jim Slater got for winning a community service award was louder than any goal celebration I had heard that year at Rexall Place in Edmonton or the Saddledome in Calgary. Simply put, the Winnipeg crowd was putting *most* other Canadian hockey crowds to shame, with the possible exception of those at the Bell Centre in Montreal. There are many skeptics out there who wonder if the Winnipeg crowds can sustain this passion, and even some Winnipeggers wonder that as well. It's a fair question.

Steven Stamkos of the Tampa Bay Lightning came into the game with fifty-nine goals and was roundly booed every single time he touched the puck, but when he actually buried number sixty, the crowd gave him a standing ovation! I had the chance to draw the winning 50/50 ticket (the purse: $55,000), and I received an incredibly warm reception when my ugly mug appeared on the Jumbotron. Dave Wheeler, a local radio guy and friend of Dan O'Toole's, was also the in-game host, and he asked me to introduce myself to the crowd. "Jon Ljungberg," I replied, to a few laughs.

The Jets didn't get the win that night, but later, in Osborne Village where I used to live, I saw tons of Jets jerseys and hats on young and old people who had just been to the game and were now unwinding with a drink or two afterward. There was no question that the team had given the city and many of the downtown businesses an economic boost.

$$\lightning$$

When the Edmonton Oilers made their unexpected run to the Stanley Cup Final back in 2006, then owner Cal Nichols made the comment that the playoff run had been good "for the soul of the city." I think everyone in Edmonton knew exactly what he meant by that. For years before a salary cap was introduced, Edmonton faced the almost constant prospect of their team leaving for a market south of the border, just as Winnipeg's team had done. Finally, after years of wondering if they would even have a team at all, fans who cared about their hockey team more than anything else in their community were able to watch the Oilers have some success again without the threat of losing them when the season was over. It made everyone in Edmonton happier, closer, and probably more productive. There is really nothing like a winning team to bring a city together.

The return of the Jets to Winnipeg was also good for "the soul of the city." A city that is still used to being the butt of jokes across the country. Maybe that's why the crowd is so loud. They don't want anyone to question their loyalty to this team. The Jets players were clearly not prepared for the reception they were given, and when the season was over, team captain Andrew Ladd remarked that players across the league had commented on how cool it was to play in front of fans like that, prompting speculation that the crowd itself might be a draw for future free agents. Let's hope so. Winnipeg is a great city, and now it's got soul again.

CHAPTER 16

Back to Toronto . . .

SEPTEMBER 11, 2001.

It started off as a regular morning on *The Big Breakfast*. We had gone to commercial break in between segments, and I noticed that a group of guests who were on the show that morning were gathering around our TV monitors in the lobby. I paid little attention to this because I had another segment to prepare for and only two minutes of commercial break time in which to do it. Suddenly Chris Albi, my trusted floor director on the show, was frantically waving her arms around in the lobby instead of prepping guests for the next segment. It wasn't a big deal because it was a cooking segment, and Chris was the kind of woman who flapped her arms constantly as she talked anyway. By then we could basically prepare for those cooking segments in our sleep. I chatted casually with the chef who was on the show that day, trying to ignore the commotion that was taking place. Suddenly with about ten seconds to go before we were back from commercial, Chris sprinted toward me and screamed, "SOMEBODY

FLEW INTO THE WORLD TRADE CENTER!" and then, with her fingers, she counted down . . . 3 . . . 2 . . . 1 . . . cue.

Needless to say I was a little taken aback. Somebody *flew* into the World Trade Center? One person? What? How could that happen? In my mind I imagined a single-engine plane piloted by some Wall Street guy who hadn't taken enough flying lessons. Had he smacked up against the exterior of one of the towers and caused a massive fire? These were the questions flying through my head as I tried to ask intelligent questions of the hard-working chef who had graciously agreed to appear on our show that morning with zero sleep. By the time the next commercial break rolled around, we had already gone off the air and started broadcasting CNN on our channel. I had been replaced by the dulcet tones of Aaron Brown.

About two weeks later I received a call from one of TSN's senior hockey producers, Rick Briggs-Jude. It was completely out of the blue. I hadn't thought much about TSN for the previous year. I was fully entrenched in the world of *The Big Breakfast*.

"How'd you like to move back to Toronto and be the first host of the NHL Network?" Rick asked.

I wasn't exactly sure what he was talking about. NHL Network? As it turned out, the league was preparing to launch its own channel and had enlisted TSN's help. The NHL would control content but the entire production crew and studios would come out of the CTV Agincourt building in Scarborough, Ontario. Plans were to do a nightly show called *NHL on the Fly*, in which the viewer would be able to see us take live "look-ins" at games for two minutes at a time. Going from game to game to game, viewers would presumably get a more complete take on what was happening in the league that night than they would by watching one game in its entirety. It was sort of the same concept as the NFL's RedZone Channel. I was intrigued but it didn't exactly sound like my dream job, and frankly it also sounded like *a lot* of work. Six hours of live television a night? I was exhausted just thinking about it, and by now I think it's pretty clear I didn't get into this business to work hard. I was also unsure of what this meant for my relationship with Darcy. I thought about it carefully, discussed it with Darcy, and others, and after plenty more careful consideration and deliberation I called Rick, thanked him for the offer, and turned it down.

For the first time in my career, I was turning down an opportunity, and a pretty good opportunity at that. This job was something that a lot of young broadcasters in my position would have killed for. But at the time, turning it down felt like the right thing to do.

Then Rick called back and offered more money.

It's a funny thing, negotiating broadcasting salaries in this country. There really isn't much of an agent system here in the world of television broadcasting unless you are *very* high up on the food chain (think Ron MacLean, Don Cherry, Frank D'Angelo). The very simple reason is that the money is not quite good enough to justify someone else taking 10 percent to negotiate for it. In fact, there is a general secrecy about what everyone is making in broadcasting unless you're working for the CBC. I had no idea what to ask for in terms of salary from the NHL Network. But when Mike Toth said "80 (thousand) would be pretty good" to start, I knew he was speaking from experience. Later I came to realize that at the time a high five-figure salary was a pretty standard starting point for sports anchors on a national level in Canada back then. It goes without saying that the Canadian broadcasting pay scale is likely a little lower than it should be simply because jobs are scarce and so many people want them. Nonetheless, I was making less than $60,000 to host a three-hour breakfast show in Winnipeg at the time, so when Rick called back and offered $78,000 for the first year, then $83,000 for the second, it felt like a bit of a windfall.

Even more than the money was the fact that I hadn't worked in sports television for two years and hadn't even been following sports as closely as I should have. Concentrating only on hockey in my transition back to sports television was a very appealing proposition because hockey was the one sport I would *never* stop following closely. One other item about the offer probably sealed the deal: Rick pointed out that after six hours of *NHL on the Fly* every night I would finish my workday by hosting a half-hour wrap-up show called *That's Hockey 2*. This wasn't the first incarnation of *That's Hockey 2*. While I was gone on my prairie sojourn, TSN had tried their own half-hour all-hockey highlight show after *Sportsdesk* that was also called *That's Hockey 2*. The show was hosted by Darren Dutchyshen and Pierre McGuire, and it was one of the very first assignments Pierre had at the network. I loved the show and the chemistry between Darren and Pierre and was shocked when TSN decided to end it after only one year on the air, though I understand that after seeing Pierre's larger-than-life personality on the show, TSN execs likely thought he needed an even bigger platform for his talents.

Nonetheless, I loved the concept of an all-hockey highlight show on TSN. I thought the network had a perfect opportunity to create another tent-pole franchise almost as important as *Sportsdesk*, just as *Baseball Tonight* was such a huge part of ESPN's lineup during the summer. But what was *really* appealing about the idea of hosting *That's Hockey 2* was the fact that it would be simulcast on TSN every night at midnight eastern. Therefore I would be on Canada's number one sports network, nationally, four nights a week at 9:00 p.m. in Vancouver, 10:00 p.m. in Calgary, 11:00 p.m. in Winnipeg, and so on. I would basically have achieved my goal of being on TSN every night.

After a tear-filled discussion with Darcy she ultimately blurted out, "I think you should go." She knew our relationship wouldn't survive my turning down this kind of opportunity. I would likely regret it and harbour resentment toward her for making me stay in Winnipeg, working for her, becoming a bit of a neutered lapdog. I called Rick back and asked for one more condition: I wanted the network to fly me back to Winnipeg once a month so I could visit Darcy and, yes, continue my relationship with her. When they agreed to my terms, I decided to accept the offer. In just three years, I had gained all the on-air experience I was going to gain by working on the prairies. Now it was time to return to the so-called centre of the Canadian media universe.

I had stupidly forgotten to ask TSN to put me up in a hotel for a few months while I found a place to live, but I had already contacted my friend Rob McDerment, a former writer with me at *Sportsdesk* who was now producing *The Reporters* with Dave Hodge. Rob graciously agreed to let me stay in an extra room in his great little house at Mount Pleasant and Davisville in midtown Toronto for about $300 a month. Rob is married now to a lovely girl named Hannah, and they had just started dating at the time. Hannah loves to tell me her very first memory of me was seeing that room, with an air mattress squeezed into it and an old floor lamp where I hung my suits, and most importantly, two large bags of Tostitos sitting on that air mattress because I had no other place to store them and they were the only food I had in the house. Welcome to the glamorous world of Canadian broadcasting.

CHAPTER 17

Park It

JUST AS WITH *The Big Breakfast*, I was clearly a last-minute desperation hire by TSN for *NHL on the Fly*. TSN was essentially running
the NHL Network, and they had stepped in and reassigned many
young writers and producers to work on the new show with just two
weeks to spare. I was the only host hired at the beginning of the network's run, but because I was working such long on-air hours, the
plan was for me to work four days on, four days off. I didn't bother to
ask them if they had a plan in place for someone else to host on the
days I wasn't working, because I was too busy getting ready to host
the show myself. I worked with several analysts in the beginning,
including former *Hockey News* editor-in-chief Steve Dryden, who
had just started full-time work at TSN; former NHL forward Dave
Reid, who had just retired that summer after winning a Stanley Cup
with the Colorado Avalanche; Canadian women's hockey star Cassie
Campbell; and perhaps most intimidating, former NHL head coach
Iron Mike Keenan, who was once again in between jobs and had
made his way back to broadcasting.

If you've followed hockey at all over the past twenty years you know that Mike Keenan has a pretty tough reputation. There are plenty of players, Brett Hull being the most obvious example, who couldn't stand playing for him. He was supposedly mean, tough, and abrasive. As usual when reputations precede people in this business, things aren't always as they seem, and off camera I found Mike to be a friendly and warm guy with a wicked sense of humour. We had a great clip of the "truck feed" from one of the games in the 2000 Stanley Cup Final. The "truck feed" is the clean version of the broadcast, directly from the broadcast truck parked outside the arena, without commercials. The talent is often still mic'd up during commercial breaks, and those of us who have access to the truck feed can hear everything they say.

The clip in question featured CBC play-by-play broadcasters Bob Cole and Harry Neale waiting for someone to bring them first-period statistics of the game they were calling so they could refer to them on the broadcast. Apparently, whoever was supposed to bring the stats to Bob and Harry had gotten lost, and Harry was not happy about it. Finally out of the blue the "runner" arrives at Bob and Harry's broadcast location, and Harry says, "Finally! The whole game we've been waiting! You fucking blockhead!"

I swear to God, over the course of the first four months of the NHL Network's existence, we played that clip on the studio monitors a hundred times, and each and every time Mike Keenan let out a big belly laugh when he heard Harry say "fucking blockhead." We even put it on a loop for him. "Fucking blockhead. Fucking blockhead. Fucking blockhead." He just loved watching Harry lose it over not having his stats sheet; he would cackle loudly each time.

There was also, as you might expect, a softer side to Mike. Like most guys who seem to have a tough exterior, their true nature comes out when their family needs them. At the same time I was hosting *The Big Breakfast* when the planes hit the World Trade

Center, Mike was frantically trying to get in touch with his daughter, who was attending Columbia University in Manhattan at the time. As for many people that day, trying to get in touch with family and friends living in New York City proved to be difficult, and after unsuccessfully trying to contact his daughter for a period of time, Mike made the decision to hop in his car and drive several hours from his cottage outside of Toronto to New York City to make sure his daughter was okay. He got as far as Niagara Falls when his daughter finally got through to him on his cell phone and assured him she was all right. I wondered what it must have been like for a father to feel that terrible sense of uncertainty behind the wheel.

⚡

As usual, I was a bundle of nerves behind the scenes, making my return to sports broadcasting on a national stage. I was nervous about my on-air performance and constantly worried that I hadn't been following hockey closely enough for this job. Looking back, I realize I was being completely irrational, but at the time I was wound up pretty tightly. One night during rehearsals for *NHL on the Fly*, I messed up a set of highlights by wrongly identifying one of the players on the scoring play. These days, I would just include such a mistake in our popular "Ya Blew It!" segment at the end of *SportsCentre*, but back then when I made a mistake like that I felt the eyes of our entire crew on me, even though our entire crew likely couldn't have cared less. I didn't yell or scream or anything, but I was clearly dejected during the commercial break, seething in angry silence. Without hesitation, Mike glanced ever so slightly over toward me and said, "Park it."

Park it. That's all he said. Suddenly I sat up straight, blood flow resumed normally, and I was ready to continue. Thanks, Coach. I guess he really did know how to motivate people.

NHL on the Fly premiered in the first week of the NHL season in the fall of 2001. After hosting five shows in which I was on television for six hours per show, I was in need of a physical and mental break. One small problem: No one had bothered to hire another host for the show. The NHL Network was doing a six-hour show on Friday night and there was no one to host it. At the time there was no TSN2, so we had even fewer on-air personalities at the network. I was asked to host one extra show to kick things off, but I had already booked a flight back to Winnipeg to visit Darcy, whom I hadn't seen in weeks. Dave Randorf was supposed to be the backup host, but he was already committed to hosting something else. I paid it no attention as it was out of my hands anyway. I flew back to Winnipeg, and Darcy and I enjoyed a night out on the town.

Once we returned home I flipped on the NHL Network to see which poor soul had been sucked in to filling in that night. To my horror, staring back at me behind the studio desk, was Dave Hodge. Yes, *the* Dave Hodge, the guy who once hosted *Hockey Night in Canada* and was now working for TSN as host of *The Reporters* as well as hosting a segment on the *NHL on TSN*. Calling Dave would have been their absolute last resort, so they clearly must have been desperate. I mean no offense to anyone working with me on that NHL Network venture, but it was clearly *beneath* Dave to have to fill in like this on a Friday night. But there he was, looking none too pleased about the matter, hosting a show for *six hours*. When he got the call at home, he apparently had a salmon in the oven and had just cracked open a bottle of white wine. I can't even imagine what that phone call must have been like.

Later, when I returned, Dave Reid, who had just started in broadcasting and was still learning the ropes, told me that Dave

Hodge was obviously upset and not thrilled about being there. Reid said he was even more nervous than usual having to work with a guy he grew up watching on *Hockey Night in Canada*. Oh, and by the way, Dave Reid had just finished playing in the Stanley Cup Final!

After about a month of Dave Randorf filling in here and there, and several auditions for other hosts that didn't work out, we finally hired a veteran auto racing reporter named Todd Lewis to be the other host of the show. Todd was an affable guy who just seemed happy to have the work, and I was thrilled that I could continue to make my somewhat ridiculous trek back to Winnipeg to see Darcy. TSN was still paying for my flights home as part of my contract, but it was becoming exhausting working four six-hour on-air shifts, then trekking out to the Hamilton airport (where WestJet flew out of at that time), flying to the 'Peg, and then returning home a day later. It was, not surprisingly, starting to take a toll on our relationship. I could see the signs that things were beginning to fray, but I was determined to make it work and even asked Darcy to marry me when she and I visited her parents for Christmas 2001. As it turned out, that wasn't really the beginning of our life together—it was the beginning of the end.

CHAPTER 18

Called Up to the Big Leagues

BACK IN TORONTO, I WAS THRIVING career-wise. I was appearing on TSN every night. The NHL even flew a crew out to the All-Star Game in Los Angeles to cover the festivities. I had a chance to interview NHL commissioner Gary Bettman back when he wasn't despised by everyone in hockey except the owners. It was amazing to be a part of a start-up network with so many young writers and producers. It was like a dream. But after the NHL season was over, I had very little work to do. We packaged together several "fill" shows for the network to run that summer that I had to host, so I couldn't just take off for July and August or anything. I was bored out of my mind most "work" days, rambling around downtown Toronto, having lunch with friends, and occasionally wandering over to the gym to half-heartedly work out. I realized I wasn't quite ready for early retirement, so I called up my old friend Mark Milliere—the same Mark Milliere who had ignored me while I stood right next to his computer years before as a writer in the newsroom. Since then Mark had ascended in the ranks of the network and was now in charge of all news and information production at TSN. He was also responsible for choosing the hosts for *SportsCentre*.

I mentioned to Mark that I was bored and that if he needed someone to fill in on *SportsCentre* while other hosts took their summer vacations, I would be more than happy to do so. I also pointed out that the network was already paying me, so I was happy to come in for work whenever he needed. I just wanted to get my face out there in front of a few more eyeballs and have something to do. Mark took note of my suggestion and I figured he might forget about it, but just two days later he called me at home and asked me to fill in the next week. Suddenly, I was filling in on several editions of the show throughout the summer and enjoying it thoroughly. I even hosted my first show with Darren Dutchyshen, a truly surreal experience to host the show I had always wanted with the broadcaster I had always admired. It was a fun summer, but I knew I was set to return to the NHL Network in the fall.

$$\frac{1}{2}$$

That fall, TSN was set to begin rebroadcasting national NHL games on their network for the first time since Sportsnet outbid them for the hockey cable package back in 1998. Sportsnet was essentially able to launch their network based on landing that cable package, and while it hadn't been devastating for TSN, there was much joy at the network when TSN won the rights back. I was among many employees at the network who participated in focus groups led by then TSN president Keith Pelley. Keith wanted to find out if there was another, better way of presenting the hockey broadcast during intermissions. CBC had a rock-solid formula with Ron and Don and the Hot Stove. Keith wanted to do something completely different from that. Problem is, hockey fans don't want something different from that. They are hockey fans. During the commercial breaks they want guys to talk about hockey.

But Keith was determined to find a better way, so months before hockey returned to the airwaves, he would corral eight to ten of us at a time into a boardroom. Keith would throw out ideas: "How about bands? What if a band played during intermission? How about a comedian? Maybe a few comedians?" It all sounded like a bad idea to me. I didn't think hockey audiences would go for it. Pretty much everyone in the focus groups I attended made it very clear that we all felt the same way. Everyone strongly suggested that TSN simply try to hire the best hockey people they could find, have them talk about hockey, and leave it at that.

The powers that be listened to our suggestion, ignored it, and then promptly brought in the puppets. Actual puppets operated by actual puppeteers that they planned to use to entertain viewers between periods. The puppets apparently cost a fortune to commission, and they consisted of two puppet buddies sitting in their basement watching the *NHL on TSN* and commenting on the game and the broadcast. In hindsight it was amazing how ballsy TSN was being with their choices. They were trying stuff. Most of it wasn't going to work, but they didn't want to do the same old thing.

And then there was Linda Freeman. Had Linda not been hired, and then subsequently fired, as TSN's new hockey host, I would never have been given the opportunity to host *SportsCentre* full time. I owe my career to her as much as anyone.

TSN wanted to hire the first female hockey host in the country's history. I thought it was a great idea. The country was absolutely ready for a female host of a major hockey broadcast, and there were definitely several worthy candidates whom TSN could have hired at the time. The network decided to go in a completely different direction and hire Linda, who had last worked as a host on CTV Vancouver's morning show and had gained most of her on-air experience at The Weather Network. She was a completely capable broadcaster, very attractive, and seemed like a good fit. She was not a hockey expert, which TSN was quick to point out, but that wasn't what TSN wanted for this job anyway. TSN needed a ringleader for their new forward-thinking intermission show. A more general host who could throw it over to the hockey experts for hockey talk but also introduce the bands and comedians and, yes, the puppets.

TSN put a ton of money behind Linda throughout the summer. Billboards all over the country featured Linda with her flowing red hair and gorgeous smile. Radio ads across the country touted her as a groundbreaker who was going to hit the airwaves that fall. TSN had invested a lot in the Linda Freeman brand. But after several weeks of rehearsals and just four days before the network's first regular-season broadcast, TSN decided it just wasn't working. Linda would continue to be involved in the broadcast as a roving reporter, and James Duthie would move from hosting the 10:00 Eastern Standard Time (EST) edition of *SportsCentre* to serve as the new host of the *NHL on TSN*. Blake Price would move from co-hosting the 11:00 Pacific Time (PT) edition of *SportsCentre* to the 10:00 EST edition. Those series of moves left Jennifer Hedger without a co-host. So many capable people were already waiting for that co-host spot in-house: David Amber, Dan Pollard, Cory Woron, all of them excellent broadcasters who really should have been given the gig. Instead, based on my two months of hosting during the summer, Mark immediately placed me next to Jennifer in the 11:00 PT slot Monday to Friday. Amazingly, the other anchors did not shun me, and they took the news with grace and class, something that could not be said about me when I didn't get the *Olympic Morning* hosting gig on CTV during the London Games. You'd think I would've learned from them.

Jay Onrait

Now I was hosting with Jennifer every day and loving it. She and I were about the same age, we got along great, and we had the same sense of humour. I knew, however, that Jen was just starting to make a huge splash on the Canadian sports broadcasting scene and that if I was to work with her for several years, I was destined to be the "guy next to the beautiful blonde on *SportsCentre.*" It was time to let my personality come out and do the show the way I had always wanted: with a mix of absurd humour and spontaneity, the same attributes I had admired in David Letterman all those years ago. I was going to change sportscasting, not necessarily for the better, and not overnight, but I was going to leave my mark.

CHAPTER 19

The Death of the Medium

TWO YEARS LATER, BLAKE PRICE returned to the west coast to raise his family in his hometown, Jennifer Hedger moved up to the 10:00 show with Dutchy, and I was paired with Dan O'Toole on the 11:00 p.m. PT edition of *SportsCentre* in a moment that many sports media critics refer to as the death of the medium in our country.

The chemistry was there right away, but the show as you know it now did not happen overnight.

Just as I had hosted my first edition of *SportsCentre* with Dutchy, Dan hosted his first edition of *SportsCentre* with me. It was not long after I started to work with Jennifer, approximately December of 2002. Dan had just joined the network after a stint in Vancouver as a sports anchor at Citytv.

Dan arrived in Toronto like every Vancouverite: lamenting the lack of scenery and ocean at their front door. I remember for the first couple of weeks I'd pass Dan at a desk in the newsroom and he'd be looking at a live camera shot of Grouse Mountain on The Weather Network website. It was pretty pathetic, actually. But I was absolutely blown away by Dan's talent during our first show together. He didn't seem nervous in the least, and his performance during that first show had me convinced he would go places at TSN. As it turns out the poor guy was going places all right: He was going to have to work with me every day.

When we were first paired together, we didn't start turning *SportsCentre* into "the Ha Ha Hut" right away. That's what Mark Milliere liked to call our show when he thought it was getting too far into the comedy realm and didn't have enough sports content for his liking. The truth is we just really like the same stuff when it comes to comedy, so when one of us came up with an idea for the show that involved Dan getting attacked by a bat drawn on cardboard attached to a string on the end of a hockey stick, we both thought that idea was hilarious and worked to convince the crew to "go with it." Up until that point, our crew (director, camera operators, technical director, and so on) was used to producing a very conventional newscast-style show: single-camera shots of the anchor reading off a teleprompter, reading highlights. You know, sportscasting.

For whatever reason, even though I knew we would alienate a large part of the audience with our shenanigans, I was utterly convinced we were taking the show in the right direction. Streaming videos on the Web was starting to take off. Soon people would have access to highlights on their tablets and phones whenever and wherever they wanted. No need to wait until 1:00 a.m. eastern time for your day's sports highlights anymore. We needed to deliver something more, give the viewers another reason to tune in. That's what led me to cut a Phantom of the Opera mask out of lined paper and sing "Music of the Night."

It was actually pretty early on in the time that Dan and I hosted the show together. You can tell by the fact that Dan has 78 percent less grey hair and looks twelve years old. We were still "figuring out the show" to a large extent, and our crew was not used to elaborate sketches being performed on what was supposed to be a traditional late-night sports highlight show.

That evening our nightly Top 10 category was "National Anthems." We had already done this Top 10 several times before with all the usual suspects: Carl Lewis butchering the American anthem at a Chicago Bulls–New Jersey Nets game ("uh-oh," he famously said after his voice cracked on a high note); Dennis (K.C.) Parks turning "O Canada" into "O Tannenbaum" at the very first Las Vegas Posse game in the Canadian Football League. This time, however, our Top 10 was inspired by a recently mangled anthem: the star of a local Baltimore production of *The Phantom of the Opera* treating the singing of the "Star-Spangled Banner" at an Orioles game like it was his audition for *American Idol*. Holding the final note for an obnoxiously long time at an obnoxiously high pitch. The crowd didn't know whether to clap or plug their ears.

Knowing that we would play this clip leading into my introduction of the Top 10, I decided to make use of my two years of musical theatre training in Athabasca, the home of all major musical theatre productions. I confiscated a black cloth "shawl" that our camera operators use to "colour correct" the TV cameras before every show (I don't know what that means either). That would be my cape. Then using skills I had acquired in kindergarten, I found a piece of regular lined paper and cut out a Phantom mask with scissors. I found several Phantom masks online and tried to draw the best one I could, poking a hole in it so I would be able to see the teleprompter. I used Scotch tape to fasten it to my hair, which would result in the painful removal of the mask moments after the shot was completed. I also soon realized that I couldn't fasten the other side of the mask to the other side of my head or it would lose its effect, so the mask sat fastened to only one side of my head like a cottage screen door that was permanently flapping in the breeze.

I tried to remember some lines from the musical to sing for the early part of the intro. My parents had taken my sister and me to the show at the Jubilee Auditorium in Edmonton, so I was somewhat familiar with the material. "Music of the niiiiiiight" and "Christine, Christine" was about the best I could come up with. Later, viewers commented that I had a nice timbre to my voice, which I really appreciated. I was no Colm Wilkinson, but it was important to get this character just right.

The intro featured me (as the Phantom) expressing outrage at the anthem singer in Baltimore, judging him "unfit to wear my mask" and dismissing his performance outright while mentioning I was a big fan of the Philadelphia Flyers' American Hockey League affiliate . . . the Phantoms.

As Dan pointed out during the intro, this was supposed to be a sports highlight show. I thought I might receive negative feedback or be told by my bosses at TSN to leave the costumes to the experts, but to my surprise and delight I heard nothing from my bosses and nothing but praise ever since from viewers. It was a bit of a TSN Turning Point in the show for us, proof that we could let these silly little ideas we had behind the scenes come to fruition on screen, breaking up the show a bit and separating ourselves from other shows of the same genre.

I started to branch out with Dan a bit more. Growing up in northern Alberta watching and following sports, my friends and I began to take special pride in athletes who played and excelled in sports most Canadians didn't traditionally excel at, like Larry Walker in Major League Baseball. Every time we'd watch Larry play outfield for the Montreal Expos and later the Colorado Rockies, we'd yell "Canadian!" in a high-pitched voice. I carried that tradition over to the show when I would voice a highlight pack and yell "Canadian!" when we featured someone like Toronto-born-and-raised Joey Votto of the Cincinnati Reds or Victoria-born-and-raised Steve Nash of the Phoenix Suns. I knew it was resonating when people started yelling "Canadian!" at me on the street. But now when I walk anywhere around Canada, the thing most people yell at me is "BOBROVSKY!"

There isn't much of a story to it. In 2010, the Philadelphia Flyers signed as their backup goaltender a twenty-two-year-old from Novokuznetsk, Russia, named Sergei Bobrovsky. The first time I heard his last name it sounded like the last name of a rogue cop on the edge from a 1970s William Friedkin–directed movie such as *The French Connection*. A cop who regularly got called into his sergeant's office and told to "turn in your badge and gun!" or he would be "off the case." That was honestly it. There was nothing else to it. So whenever Bobrovsky got some rare playing time, I would ask Producer Tim to let me read the highlight package so I could come up with a different way of describing Bobrovsky every time ("You're an embarrassment to the force, Bobrovsky!"). For whatever reason, this may go down as the most famous thing I ever do in my career. Two seasons later, Bobrovsky was traded to Columbus and became a sensation, putting together a Vezina Trophy–winning season with the Blue Jackets and landing on the cover of video game boxes. I was subsequently given much undeserved credit for the young goaltender's success, even though, to this day, I have still never met the man.

We were having fun. Our show repeated over and over in the morning the next day, so if we made a mistake we would have to fix it before it ran incorrectly another ten times. Eventually we realized it was a lot easier to create a segment where we simply acknowledged those mistakes. It would save us time and effort and potentially deliver a few laughs. That's how our "Ya Blew It!" segment was born, where we simply list our errors at the end of the show and apologize for them. We called it "Ya Blew It!" as a tribute to two of our comedy heroes, Tim and Eric. Tim Heidecker used the line during one of their sketches on *Tim and Eric Awesome Show, Great Job!* It seemed like the perfect title.

People started to take notice of what Dan and I were doing, and we gained a little bit of a following. Mark Milliere's idea was that because our late-night show repeated several times in the morning, kids would grow up watching us and continue to watch us as they got older, presumably ending up by tuning in at college when they returned from the bar late at night. It worked. We started to get people coming up to us on the streets telling us we were a major part of their childhood. Working with Dan was easy and fun. It didn't feel like work. It still doesn't.

CHAPTER 20

Fear the Beard

AT ONE POINT DURING the first couple of years Dan and I hosted the show together, I decided it would be a good idea for me to try to wear a beard on air.

The list of on-air television personalities with beards is surprisingly small: Wolf Blitzer, Charley Steiner, the Most Interesting Man in the World, and so on. I could always grow a nice beard and mustache, and I thought it might be another way to set myself apart, or maybe I was just bored. Either way, I wanted to give the beard a shot. I had taken a week-long vacation and returned to work with a somewhat healthy growth on my face that might best be described as "George Michael in the 'Faith' era."

My idea was simple: I had to host an 8:00 p.m. EST update on TSN, I would have the beard on during the update, and if the producer at the time or anyone else thought it looked horrible I would just shave it off. I brought my razor and shave cream with me to the network that night, so I was ready for the worst. I hosted the update, and while I didn't look *bad* I also needed a few more days of growth to really let it fill in and look acceptable. The producer at the time, Mark Blimke, sat down beside me after the update and we both agreed I should shave it off. Just as I was about to leave for the washroom, the newsroom phone rang and someone called out, "Jay, it's for you."

I picked up the phone at my desk.

"Jay, it's Phil King."

Phil King was the president of TSN at the time.

"Uh, hey, Phil," I replied. This was *highly* unusual. No network president had ever called in to the newsroom before at any point during my time there as a writer or a broadcaster. Newsroom and on-air issues fell under the domain of the vice-president of production.

"What's going on with your face there?" he asked.

"Oh, you know, just tried to grow a bit of a beard but I don't think it looked very good. I was just heading to the bathroom to shave it off."

"I saw it. I think shaving it off is a really good idea. Have a great night, Jay."

He has never called the newsroom since.

Embarrassing as that was, it paled in comparison to the time Marek Malik threatened to kill me.

About three or four years into our run on *SportsCentre* I was reading a set of basketball highlights when I saw on the script "MAREK MALIK AND HIS SON COURTSIDE." Malik was a defenceman for the New York Rangers at the time, and he had taken his son to a Knicks game at Madison Square Garden. In the greatest act of stupidity in my short life (and that's saying something), upon seeing a shot of Malik and his red-haired son on our studio monitor I blurted out on live television, "There's Marek Malik and his red-headed stepchild!" Not funny, not smart, and overall just *ill-advised*. I nonetheless waved off suggestions from Tim and Dan that we re-record the segment for our morning reruns, thinking that Malik himself would never see it and no one would care anyway.

The next day I awoke to an e-mail from our senior producer. Turns out the Rangers watched our show in the dressing room before the morning skate at Madison Square Garden. In fact, it turned out that pretty much every team in the league watched us before their morning skate. The idea that my words were not accountable was suddenly thrown in my face. The producer informed me that Malik had heard what I said and was "extremely upset" and was "threatening to do something about it." This was of deep concern to me. I didn't have Dominique Bosshart around to protect me now.

Luckily, the aforementioned Pierre McGuire knew Malik and was able to contact him and convince him not to come after me like Liam Neeson in *Taken*. I basically avoided a well-deserved beatdown for my stupidity because I have good friends in the business who look out for me on occasion. Lesson learned. You never know who is watching.

↯

Sometime around 2004 I was asked if I might be interested in hosting the Red Bull Crashed Ice event in Quebec City. If you're not familiar with the event, it can basically be boiled down to "roller derby on ice skates down a steep hill." Only the most insane thrillseekers choose to participate. Red Bull has achieved tremendous success with these extreme sports events, and Crashed Ice was sort of the pinnacle. It had appeared on another network before, but this year TSN was picking up the broadcast and wanted me to go to Quebec City to serve as host and give the play-by-play alongside future *Hockey Night in Canada* fixture P.J. Stock. We arrived on a Friday in the middle of January when Quebec was absolutely freezing cold. The event was scheduled to take place on NHL All-Star Weekend.

Red Bull had apparently approved of my involvement, thinking that somehow my slightly bizarre style fit with their slightly bizarre "sports" event. Not surprisingly, the city was frozen that weekend, and soon after I arrived, upon realizing that my laceless John Varvatos Chuck Taylors might not have the warmth and grip necessary to navigate the streets of downtown Quebec, I ducked into a footwear store, picked out a big pair of Sorels, and charged them to the network.

The event itself was an absolute blast. Hundreds of men and women had shown up from all over the world to participate. They would fly down the custom-made track in groups of four, bumping and shoving each other along the way but mostly just trying to stay upright. P.J. decided to try out the track himself and found it a humbling experience, falling flat on his stomach after the first steep decline past the starting gate. Not that I'm calling him out or anything, as I conveniently "forgot my skates" and didn't make a run down the track at all. I feared I would lose my footing and go crashing into a pop-up poutine shack, scalding my pasty skin with hot gravy and cheese curds.

Red Bull Crashed Ice was another example of my not handling stress well. It was our first year hosting the event, and although everyone working was highly experienced in live mobile production, it wasn't a wholly TSN-produced event, so many issues were out of the hands of my show producer and director. Instead of having our own camera operators set up along the track, every network broadcasting the event was taking shots from the same group of camera operators, a clever cost-saving device to be sure, but it left us at the mercy of the one crew who was set up on the track.

Communication was also a bit of a nightmare. Trying to talk to my producer over my headset was problematic at best, but the worst part was that the skaters were all wearing identical jerseys, making it virtually impossible to tell them apart. Suddenly, I had great sympathy for Bob Cole's inability to remember names of players in his advanced age. This was my first shot at TV play-by-play, and I was up against it in a big way. I started to act petulant, demanding more communication from the producer in the truck and asking for changes to the jerseys. My complaints fell on deaf ears for the most part. These guys didn't have time to address my concerns at this point. The race was about to start, and we were showing it on television no matter how difficult it would be for me to do my job.

I started to get a bit depressed and sullen, returning to my room at the Hotel 71 to take a long hot shower and contemplate whether I'd get fired if I hopped on a plane and hightailed it out of there. It was at that point that I e-mailed Dan.

Just as Mike Keenan had managed to calm my nerves by uttering the words "Park it" a couple of years previously at the NHL Network, Dan seemed to understand just what to say.

"No matter how stressful the situation, losing your temper or freaking out about it isn't going to make it better. It's going to make it worse. It's Red Bull Crashed Ice, not the Stanley Cup Final. Just go out and have fun. If you make mistakes, you make mistakes. Who cares?"

The thing was, *I cared.* I still didn't know exactly which direction my career was going to go at that point. In my mind there was still a chance TSN would see me host Red Bull Crashed Ice, be completely dazzled at my play-calling ability, and beg to send me to the odd Thursday night NHL game between the Panthers and Blue Jackets. This was never in the cards, but in my mind I still felt like I was actually auditioning. Still, Dan's words soothed my frayed nerves somewhat, and I was able to get through the broadcast with a lot of help from P.J., who clearly had a ton of talent. Yet I could never shake the feeling that the producer and director who had been assigned to the event would forever see me as something I never, ever wanted to be seen as: high-maintenance talent.

Thanks to a heavy dose of Catholic guilt running through my veins, any outburst on set during a broadcast is immediately followed by deep regret between my two ears. Dan has formulated a pretty impressive way to calm me down in those moments when he's the one sitting next to me and he sees me about to go off like vintage Bill O'Reilly: He distracts me like a small child. Like the small child I still am in a lot of ways. He's got experience at this kind of thing because he's a father, the father of two infant daughters. So when he sees me start to go off the deep end, instead of muttering "Park it," he distracts me by bringing up something completely unrelated:

JAY: I can't believe I fucked up those Marlins highlights. Goddammit!

DAN: Did you see *Walking Dead* the other night? What a show!

And then I start to laugh. It works every time.

The truth is that in this business, for what I do every day, so much rides on your getting along with your co-anchor. We are asking a lot for people to sit and watch us on television when they could get the same highlights on the Internet. If the chemistry between the two anchors is bad, or worse, if the two anchors clearly do not like each other, absolutely no one is going to want to watch. Remember when they paired Dan Rather with Connie Chung on the *CBS Evening News*? Neither do I. There is no "train wreck factor" to watching local or national news or sports anchors who do not like each other. Viewers will just turn away. Trying to get along with someone at work whom you don't like is difficult enough. Trying to do that while pretending to like the person in front of thousands and thousands of people is truly daunting. I've always believed the audience can see right through it.

That's what makes working with Dan such a treat. It really is just like hanging out with your pal and chatting about sports. Your cheap, lovable pal who is obsessed with sunflower seeds.

Dan is also a dealmaker. We had filled in for our good friend James Cybulski on his afternoon show on TSN Radio in Toronto a few times and enjoyed it. We filled in for an entire week once, acting like our usual immature selves until the day Canadian freestyle skier Sarah Burke died unexpectedly in a training session. The news got out seconds after our radio show started, so we were forced to spend the first two hours of the show discussing it and interviewing people connected with her, including CTV's own Brian Williams. Rob Gray, who was program director of TSN Radio, was impressed that we could actually handle ourselves in a serious news situation, and I think we managed to gain a modicum of respect from him.

Dan bugged Rob as well as our bosses to allow us to do a weekly podcast in the wake of the success of shows like *The B.S. Report with Bill Simmons* and *The Rich Eisen Podcast* and *Marek vs. Wyshynski*.

We started the podcast in September of 2012 and it was an instant hit. We went to number one on iTunes right away. It was really gratifying to have instant success because the podcast is even more "out there" than the TV show is. Just an hour of unscripted talk about "butt chugging" (the art of ingesting alcohol into one's anus); stories from Producer Tim, whose voice was modulated to sound like a guy from the witness protection program; and lots and lots of talk about poop. As in feces. It's not as if we planned to become a podcast that was best known for discussions about excrement. It just sort of happened. We're not even "potty humour" types. Our friend and Our Lady Peace drummer Jeremy Taggart became a well-loved regular on the show. I genuinely enjoy doing the podcast every single week with Dan. That chemistry that we had on the desk and just our general friendship translated into something totally unique and surprisingly listenable.

You know those times when you stop and examine your life situation and say, "I'm going to miss this someday"? That's how I feel about working with Dan.

CHAPTER 21

The Blades of Glory *Junket*

THESE WERE THE BEST OF TIMES at *SportsCentre*. Our bosses were starting to become comfortable with the idea of Dan and me adding comic elements to what was supposed to be a straight-forward sports news show. If we ever took things too far we'd be politely asked to "dial it back 10 percent." Such a request would usu-ally come after we hurled confetti in the air or had one of our writ-ers appear with a chicken mask on his head. Overall, however, we were given amazing freedom to do what we wanted, and Producer Tim begrudgingly allowed himself to become a part of the show via nightly ridicule. Life was good.

Still, I wanted to get out in the field a bit and actually cover sports once in a while, so beginning in 2005 I asked and was granted the privilege of covering the NBA Finals for *SportsCentre*. I did it for the next three years, the most memorable moment coming when I suddenly found myself to be the first reporter in the Miami Heat dressing room immediately after they clinched their first NBA championship in 2006. Jason "White Chocolate" Williams soaked me with champagne as I made a futile attempt to ask him intelligent questions while taking elbows to the ribs from cranky print broadcasters. I was also sent on the road a few times to host Toronto Raptors broadcasts on TSN with Leo Rautins, back when the broadcasters covering the team actually travelled on the team plane. I was sitting happily enjoying my ice cream sundae on the way back to Toronto from Philadelphia in 2008 when suddenly I heard then Raptors head coach Sam Mitchell say loudly, "Who the hell is this peckerwood?" to everyone on the plane as he walked the aisle.

"Boy, I feel sorry for whomever *he's* talking about," I said to myself as I scooped up another bite of caramel. Leo was sitting behind me, and I turned around to ask him whom Mitchell was referring to. The look on his face said it all. *He's talking about you, idiot.* Sam then went on a diatribe about this new "peckerwood" who had suddenly appeared on his plane out of nowhere to everyone who was interested in listening. No one was listening. They had all heard this song and dance before. Realizing his "bit" was played out, Sam offered a fist for me to bump, which I promptly did, and then returned to his coaching staff to probably discuss ways to keep Primož Brezec off the court as much as possible.

After that I mostly stayed behind the desk where I belonged. However, I did cover a press junket for the network once. I've been to only one junket, and that was enough for me.

For the uninformed (consider yourselves blissfully uninformed), a "junket" is when all the major movie stars of an upcoming motion picture are gathered into a suite, or several suites, at a beautiful hotel in New York or Los Angeles. This way, different entertainment reporters from across the country and around the world can travel to that location and interview each of the stars one or two at a time. It's a subject that Billy Crystal tackled in his horrifically bad film *America's Sweethearts*. Didn't see it? Again, consider yourself blissfully lucky.

TSN had sent reporters to press junkets before, mostly for sports movies like *Cinderella Man* or *Ali*. This time they decided it might be a fun idea to send someone to the junket for a sports comedy like my favourite movie of all time: *Caddyshack*. Could you imagine working the *Caddyshack* junket? You would have had the chance to interview Michael O'Keefe, who played Danny Noonan, before he dropped off the face of the earth.

The movie in consideration for TSN coverage was *Blades of Glory* starring Will Ferrell, Jon Heder, Amy Poehler, and Will Arnett. Technically, it *was* a sports movie, though it was about as much a sports movie as *D2: The Mighty Ducks*. I loved Ferrell on *Saturday Night Live* as much as everyone else on the planet. In my mind, Ferrell's cast, including Darrell Hammond and the criminally underrated Chris Parnell, had erased the memories of a few down seasons on the show (sadly those "down seasons" pretty much involved every season with former *Kids in the Hall* star and beloved Canadian Mark McKinney).

Ferrell was also coming off *Old School* and *Anchorman* and was pretty much the hottest comedy star on the planet at the time. My bosses asked if I was interested in travelling to L.A., interviewing the entire cast of the movie, staying overnight, and then flying back the next day. Yes, I was interested. But truthfully, I was kind of terrified. I didn't really want to interview any of these people. I genuinely felt bad about their situation: Who the hell would want to sit there all day while reporters from places such as Toronto fed them dumb questions like "So how long have you been wanting to work with Jon?" The whole thing was just nauseating to me. I really had an uncomfortable feeling about it. But a trip to L.A. did sound pretty good.

I arrived in L.A. the day before the junket. All the entertainment reporters who had been invited to the junket were scheduled to get picked up at the hotel and taken to the Grove to see the film that evening. If you haven't been to L.A., the Grove is a beautiful outdoor shopping mall and another reason to hate people who get to live in that city. We would see the film with our fellow reporters, thereby giving us all the material we would need to ask the actors highly provocative and fascinating questions the following day.

It didn't take me long to realize I was the only person in the group of reporters attending the film who didn't know anyone else. These people had probably worked alongside each other on a million of these junkets. Everybody was so chummy, talking about interviews they had just done or were about to do, trading stories about recent interviews that had gone horribly wrong, and sharing general entertainment-biz gossip. I immediately felt the same way I used to feel when my parents made me attend hockey school in the Okanagan during my summer vacation as a kid. I'd arrive knowing absolutely no one because I was from Alberta, and all the other local kids would be chatting and goofing around because they had known each other for years from playing minor hockey.

So as I sat amid those reporters like an outcast that day, I did what everyone does in that situation and pretended I was reading and typing very important things into my BlackBerry, all the while my fellow film attendees relaxed and chatted like it was some sort of entertainment reporter family reunion.

I wasn't entirely concerned about looking like an outsider in this situation, however. I was already preoccupied with what I was going to ask Will Ferrell the next day. More specifically I was preoccupied with how I was going to come up with something "funny" for him to do that would justify TSN's giving me the assignment in the first place.

The film itself was just okay. I remember thinking I probably laughed more than I would have had I seen it in a theatre in Toronto in another attempt to show what a great time I was having. The premise was sort of brilliant: Two male singles figure skaters are banned from competing individually, but a brilliant figure skating coach (played by "Coach" himself, Craig T. Nelson) figures out a loophole that allows them to compete as a pair. Hilarity ensues. Probably the best gimmick was having then real-life husband and wife Will Arnett and Amy Poehler play a brother and sister figure skating duo with designs on bringing down our heroes, Ferrell and Heder. In the end I thought the film was missing a little something. Ferrell would tackle the world of ABA basketball (*Semi-Pro*) and NASCAR racing (*Talladega Nights*) to greater success in the future.

After the movie was over, I imagine the rest of the entertainment reporter mafia went to some sort of fashionable lounge in West Hollywood to swap stories about how difficult it was to interview Tommy Lee Jones or something. I quickly hopped in a cab and went straight back to the hotel to plan my interview strategy. I had one specific plan: I knew my interview time itself would be no longer than five minutes (as it turned out it was four minutes). Therefore, I needed to allot my time accordingly. My first idea was to have Ferrell himself participate in "Headlines," which was the voiced-over montage that kicked off every edition of *SportsCentre*. Usually this involved Dan O'Toole or me reading a script that said something like this:

"Coming up on *SportsCentre* . . . The Leafs try to knock the crown off the Kings in Los Angeles . . . PLUS . . . The Oilers head to Minnesota to try to TAME the Wild! . . . AND . . . The RED HOT Flames travel to the music city . . . to TANGLE with the Predators!"

The script never really deviated much. The key was to tell the viewer what was coming up on the show using clever wordplay that related to the teams playing that night. Simple. So my thought was: What if I could get Ferrell to read the opening headlines to the show in which my story would appear? Surely that alone would justify my entire trip to Los Angeles! I could just imagine the reaction back in Toronto!

"Brilliant work, Onrait!" they'd say. "We're doubling your salary immediately!"

The question was: Would Ferrell play along? Or would he actually be so tired of answering question after mundane question from a continuous series of entertainment talking heads that he would be cranky and shut down my idea on the spot? I decided I simply had to go for it and hope for the best. What I didn't count on was the fact that I wouldn't be interviewing him alone.

Often in the case of ensemble pictures with several so-called stars, they will pair a couple of stars together to save time. The idea is that you're probably going to ask the same questions to Will Arnett that you're going to ask Amy Poehler, *so why not have them in the same room answering those questions together*? I'm sure for people like Poehler and Arnett it's also a welcome proposition since it means they won't be completely bored the entire day since they'll have someone to talk to. For the reporters asking the questions it's also appreciated because perhaps the stars will loosen up and banter about the film and play off each other a bit. For me, it was a bit of a nightmare. I had envisioned being alone with Ferrell in a room, connecting with the guy over sports (he had said often in interviews that he was a huge sports fan and actually considered becoming a sportscaster while attending USC), having him laugh uproariously over my ideas, maybe even asking me to join him on the set of his next film. Oh, the fun we would have!

The next morning I woke early, ordered room service oatmeal (easy on my notoriously bad stomach), and went over my questions for all the actors I'd be interviewing. Most importantly, I had collected all the information I needed for Ferrell to participate in the headlines portion of the show. And by "information I collected" I mean I wrote his "script" on a Post-it-note-sized piece of hotel stationery. There were no lines in the script for Ferrell to read, all I had written down was this:

LEAFS–THRASHERS

OILERS–BLUE JACKETS

FLAMES–KINGS

BLADES OF GLORY!

That's it. That's what I was going to present to this beloved, highly successful comedy actor: a piece of paper with ten words on it that really made no sense whatsoever.

Coincidentally, there happened to be another press junket going on in the hotel at the same time for a serious film called *Reign Over Me*, starring Adam Sandler, Don Cheadle, Liv Tyler, and Jada Pinkett Smith. The entire hotel was bursting at the seams with reporters, publicists, and hangers-on. It was exciting but at the same time it did little to calm my nerves. I threw on a suit and headed up to the *Blades of Glory* junket, only to find myself sharing an elevator with Tyler and Pinkett Smith, who were heading up to be interviewed in their own junket. Tyler looked tired, but Pinkett Smith was positively radiant, much more beautiful than I had ever seen her on the silver screen. Both ladies were surrounded by their teams of managers and handlers, and an awkward silence was thankfully broken when I jumped off on my floor to start my day. They were probably thinking this was going to be the worst day of their lives.

When I arrived on my floor for the *Blades* junket I was briefed on the situation: I would be interviewing Craig T. Nelson first, alone, followed by Arnett and Poehler together, and then Ferrell and Heder *together*.

My heart sank.

How would I explain to Heder that I needed him to sit and be quiet while Ferrell worked his comedy magic for me? I decided it was too late to change the plan. Just like everyone, I liked Heder in *Napoleon Dynamite*, but I knew that Ferrell alone would knock the opening headlines out of the park. Hopefully, Heder wouldn't be too offended. Maybe he would appreciate the break after the assembly line of banal questions.

I waited my turn in one suite that had been designated the "wait-your-turn suite." I sat silently and went over my questions for Coach. Anyone who glanced over at me would have seen I was noticeably terrified. I had never in my life seen a single episode of *Coach*. That's right, not one single episode. As I panicked about my first interview of the day, I overhead two of the entertainment scribblers mention that Nelson was a "tough interview." Great. Just the way I wanted to start my day. My name was called and I was led into another suite where Nelson sat, alone, chatting amiably with the camera operator and lighting guy.

As I mentioned previously, each interviewer was given an allotted time of four minutes. This may seem like a short amount of time, and if the interview is going well, that's absolutely true. But if the interview is going poorly, it seems like an eternity. I was immediately transported back to my days on *The Big Breakfast* where every single segment on the show was four minutes without exception. Interview with an author? Four minutes. Cooking a crepe with a local chef? You'd better cook that crepe in four minutes. Band playing a song? That song needs to be around three minutes and thirty seconds if you want me to take thirty seconds to tell the viewing audience what bar you'll be playing at that night.

Every time you walked into a suite to interview one of the actors, your name and affiliation were announced as if you were competing in a beauty pageant. "Jay On-RAYTE, TSN," said the person in charge. Nelson took one look at me and said a dismissive "hello" and we were off. I thought that maybe I should start by asking him a somewhat serious question about the film even though it was a comedy, because I imagined that Nelson was the kind of actor who took his craft seriously no matter what the genre. So I started with "You've obviously done comedy before to great success, but this movie was kind of absurd, not exactly what we're used to seeing from you. What made you decide to sign on for a Will Ferrell movie?" (BRILLIANT, ONRAIT.)

He stared straight at me and said nothing. After the most uncomfortable five-second pause in my life, he replied, "Well, why not?"

"Yeah, good question," I said.

Silence.

"Uh," I muttered. "So, you a big figure skating fan?"

He laughed. A genuine actual hearty laugh! My strategy had worked! Convince him that I had absolutely no idea what I was doing (no problem there) and hope he would take sympathy on me and see that I wasn't another one of those fake-hair, fake-teeth entertainment cattle that he would be facing throughout the day.

The final two minutes of the interview were a bit of a blur. I believe I asked him about the plausibility of two male figure skaters forming an ice-dancing team and whether it's something he would actually watch. I think he had already tuned me out at that point, but the truth is I had absolutely no intention of using any of this material for my finished story anyway. Unless he said something brilliantly profound, which he didn't. I was just happy he didn't reach over and punch me. I suppose if he had, that *definitely* would have made the story.

Next, I was instructed to head across the hall to another suite where Amy Poehler and Will Arnett sat waiting for my brilliant and poignant questions. Amy is well known as a former *Saturday Night Live* cast member and the star of the flat-out brilliant *Parks and Recreation*, a show that is very likely an unrealistic depiction of what it's like to work in a parks and rec office in a small Midwestern city. However, since I've never worked in civic administration, I'm not bothered by it and can enjoy the show as the instant classic that it is. Also, the character of Ron Swanson (played by Nick

Offerman) wears a moustache that is the inspiration for my duster every Movember.

Arnett was one of the stars of the equally brilliant *Arrested Development*. Not to mention the fact that he is a born-and-raised Torontonian and has stated often that he is a huge Maple Leafs fan and that Wendel Clark is his favourite player. I wasn't really planning on working that angle in the interview, but then I entered the room and they announced my name and affiliation: "Jay On-RAT, TSN."

"TSN? I love TSN!" said Arnett.

"He *loves* hockey," said Poehler.

Thank you, TSN!

What followed was practically a lovefest for all things hockey: "Every Saturday night he watches Don Cherry," said Poehler.

"He's on another network; we won't be talking about *him*," I replied, to uproarious laughter from my interviewees. *Uproarious laughter! Maybe I should be doing the whole story about these two wonderful people*, I thought to myself. We didn't even talk about *Blades of Glory* and I didn't care. The fact that Arnett was talking non-stop about the Leafs and Poehler was playing along was a perfect angle for a sports-network reporter to take on a story like this. They had already made the day a success.

The only disaster came at the end.

Like many people, when I get nervous my palms get sweaty. It's a curse. The area under my nose where I would grow a mustache also gets sweaty, which is a bizarre thing and highly embarrassing. Dan calls it my "coke lip." The sweaty-palms thing is easy to hide unless you're about to shake hands with two actors following a highly successful and enjoyable interview. As the end of the interview approached I thought about wiping my palms on my pants, but it was impossible to do so in a subtle way. Believe it or not I also seriously considered giving both of them the Howie Mandel fist-tap that he gives everyone because he is a germaphobe. I probably should have gone that route, but I thought it was just too weird at the time. Instead, I offered my sweaty palm to Will, who shook it without hesitation. Guys obviously notice this stuff and find it gross, but I think he was still on a high from talking about the Leafs. Amy wasn't so easily distracted. I reached out my hand in all its clammy glory and her smile immediately turned into a frown. I made Amy Poehler frown with my sweaty palms. Oh, well.

And then it was on to Will Ferrell . . .

Whisked down the hallway with surprising speed (they likely were on to the fact that I didn't belong there and wanted me out as soon as possible), I entered another suite, where Ferrell and Jon Heder sat side by side chatting pleasantly. Once again my TSN affiliation worked to my advantage . . .

"Jay On-RAY, TSN."

Ferrell perked up.

"I've seen you," he said.

"Yeah?" I replied, trying to contain my excitement.

"You're on TSN?"

"Yup, I host the late-night *SportsCentre.*"

"Right! Right! That's the one with the one guy in Vancouver and the other guy in Toronto, and you have the two screens . . . I've seen you!" Ferrell was getting genuinely excited at this point and turned to Heder. "When I was filming *Superstar* in Toronto I would watch TSN every night!"

I didn't have the heart, desire, or time to correct him at that moment, but I understood exactly what he was saying. Back in the late '90s *SportsCentre* (then called *Sportsdesk*) tried an experiment to appeal to viewers on the west coast. This was another futile attempt to placate viewers in the rest of the country who were convinced our network's initials actually stood for *Toronto Sports Network* because of our heavy-handed coverage of the Maple Leafs.

The network bought a studio in Vancouver, and every night during the 11:00 PT show we would feature two anchors on the screen linked via satellite, one from the Vancouver studio and one from the Toronto studio. The experiment was short lived, and a couple of years later the studio was actually sold to Sportsnet. That's where Vancouver sportscasting legend Don Taylor hosts his show to this day.

"Or maybe I saw you when I was in Montreal," continued Ferrell, working it out in his head. *Blades of Glory* had been partially filmed in Montreal, and the entire cast had spent months of the past winter there, making it entirely possible that Ferrell had seen me while getting ready to start his day or even late at night. Either way, the ice had been broken and we were off. For my second straight interview we barely spoke of the movie. The entire four minutes was spent talking about how *Sportsdesk* was now *SportsCentre*, just like ESPN but spelled *C-e-n-t-r-e* instead of *C-e-n-t-e-r*. (Believe it or not Heder also seemed genuinely interested in this). I also asked Ferrell about his aborted sportscasting career. "I did think about it," he said.

"Really?" asked Heder, who was unsurprisingly unconcerned that I was basically ignoring him.

There was one person working in the room whose sole job was to tell you how much time you had left in the interview. We quickly reached the "one-minute" mark, and I knew I needed to pitch my idea for him to read the opening headlines. So I explained my plan, knowing he would be familiar with the concept, having watched so much *SC* over the years. I handed him my small piece of hotel stationery with the various team matchups on it and then told him to say whatever he wanted about *Blades* at the end. He took one look at the paper, smiled, laughed quietly to himself, and then looked directly into the camera and said this:

"Hi, I'm Will Ferrell, and welcome to *SportsCentre* here on TSN! C-E-N-T-R-E [mock disgust] . . . Today we've got some exciting Leafs–Thrashers action! As we chase for the Cup! [points at me off-camera and smirks] That's followed by the Oilers and Blue Jackets, and then it's the Flames and probably the best team in the NHL . . . the Los Angeles Kings [the Kings were the worst team in the NHL at the time and Ferrell was keenly aware of this], plus an exclusive look at my new movie, *Blades of Glory*—thanks!"

I was in awe. The guy could have blown me off completely and told me he wasn't interested in doing my shtick. He and Heder could have laughed in my face and told me to take my hotel stationery back to Canada with me. Instead, Ferrell seemed to get genuine enjoyment out of the whole exercise like it was some sort of welcome creative break to his day. It was a huge relief. I left Ferrell and Heder with sweaty handshakes and said my goodbyes to the Paramount staffers working the junket.

I ran into former *Good Rockin' Tonite* host Terry David Mulligan in the lobby as I was checking out of the Beverly Hills Hotel. Terry wanted to have a drink later that afternoon, but I had already planned to head down to Santa Monica, find a cheap motel, and spend a couple of days living like a beach bum. I found a place that looked and smelled like it hadn't been renovated since 1974. It happened to be just down the street from the Zephyr Surf Shop where the original Z-Boys skateboard team used to hang out, a fascinating bit of trivia for a guy like me who used to try to pretend he was a skateboarder. It was perfect.

I was still pretty wound up from the whole junket experience, so I managed to secure a small amount of much-appreciated marijuana from a shady character on the Venice Beach strip. I had heard that the Venice strip was the place to buy drugs locally, since I wasn't about to trek to downtown Los Angeles. Ignoring the fact that getting arrested for purchasing marijuana in a foreign country that I had travelled to on the company dime might not be the best thing for my career, I took a walk down to the famous muscle beach just after checking in to my fleabag palace. It didn't take long for my darting eyes to catch the attention of a guy about my age wearing a backpack on a bench just off the beach. He took one look at me and called out, "Hey, Tom Hanks!"

Weed secured soon after, I returned to the much less sketchy Santa Monica strip, parked myself on the beach, and mentally checked out for a few days.

The *Blades of Glory* feature itself turned out just okay. I tried to include Gino Reda in the piece for comedic purposes. Gino was a regular host during the show's Vancouver–Toronto satellite days, so I thought I could tie it in to Ferrell's comment about watching the show in that format. Gino has long been a source of comedy for us on our show, and he's been very good-natured about it. Unfortunately, in the case of this story I think my inclusion of Gino unintentionally came across as snarky and mean, and I really regret it. I don't exactly think my bosses loved the piece either since they never bothered to send me on another junket. It's probably just as well. The next time I tried to buy weed on the Venice Beach strip, I probably would have been arrested by an undercover agent and accused of setting up a Canadian drug ring. I can see the headline now: "Tom Hanks Doppelganger Thwarted." I think it's probably for the best that I stick to my natural studio habitat.

But whenever I catch Ferrell in a movie these days, I always remember how nice he was about my stupid little piece of hotel stationery.

CHAPTER 22

Sexually Harassed by a Senior Citizen

WHEN I WOULD FINALLY DRAG my stuffy ass into the TSN studios in beautiful Scarborough, Ontario, my first stop every night was the makeup chair.

I should qualify that statement: The first stop of the night was the Shell station up the road. Dan and I have a *slight* addiction to energy drinks.

How do I know it's an addiction? Because despite the fact that it's very likely killing me at a slow pace, I have no intention of stopping anytime soon. I imagine that drinking a king-size beer can of citrus-flavoured NOS five minutes before the show is a little like what it would have been like for John Belushi to perform high on cocaine on *Saturday Night Live* back in the late '70s. I'm sure it's not affecting the way we host the show at all. Let's just say we were lucky that drug testing for Bell employees didn't include taurine.

I also realize I'm taking a risk by devoting an entire chapter of this book to the art and practice of applying and wearing makeup as a necessity for my job, but I'm good with it if you are. I wear makeup every single night I go to work. There's no shame in that, is there? Would it make you feel any better if I told you watching me on television without makeup would be a bit like watching Vincent Price host *SportsCentre* on his deathbed? Too harsh? Just thought that might put things in perspective. The truth is, those studio lights are powerful, and you need makeup just to look *normal* and not completely washed out. I always appreciated the fact that I spent most of my on-air career in a studio as opposed to being a field reporter, where my pale skin and dark circles would likely have distracted viewers from everything I was saying. All you aspiring reporters now know the most important element to a successful career in the field: perfect skin.

I am a man who loves sports and I wear makeup. I don't think these things need to be mutually exclusive. Whether you realize it or not, men have been wearing makeup in the sports and entertainment industries for years. Let's think of a few examples. Oh, I just did. And then I wrote them down:

Think about all the football and baseball players who wear eyeblack under their eyes on hot summer days. If anything, it's become a symbol of masculinity. Plus it gave Tim Tebow another place to display John 3:16, and we all know how important that is to Tim. How about the superstars of wrestling? The Road Warriors, Animal and Hawk, wouldn't have been quite so fierce had they come into the ring without any war paint. Sting wouldn't have had any gimmick whatsoever; he'd be a guy ripping off the lead singer of the Police. And don't even get me started on the Ultimate Warrior. Can you imagine the Ultimate Warrior without makeup? He would have just been a bulked-up dude with a mullet. In other words, he would have looked like quite a few people I went to high school with in Alberta. How about Bowie? Or the New York Dolls? Or Poison? Or Boy George? (I probably should have stopped with Poison.)

When I got my first on-air job as the sports director at Global

Saskatoon, I didn't even realize I would *have* to wear makeup on television. They certainly didn't teach us that at Ryerson. I realize I probably should have known this on my own, but as I mentioned before I've never been a big "details" guy. My co-anchor in Saskatoon, Corey Ginther, was kind enough to take me under his wing right before my first broadcast and give me a few quick tips: Dab a bit of powder under the eyes and on the forehead, cover up the beard, make sure you haven't missed any zits or razor burn marks. Had someone been able to film that moment in my life, it would have been the closest thing to watching two drag queens discovering their craft for the first time.

The following year I was hosting *The Big Breakfast* in Winnipeg, and by then I knew my way around a container of pressed powder. A year of makeup application had not exactly turned me into Oscar winner Rick Baker, but I could at least do a credible job of covering up my mug and making it slightly less hideous. Dragging my ass out of bed at 5:30 in the morning in the freezing Manitoba cold made me grateful for my newly acquired makeup skills. I was fairly certain Winnipeggers didn't want to wake up to a show hosted by a guy looking like a hobo who had just robbed a liquor store. Especially when that hobo was wearing clothes rejected by the Backstreet Boys. I'm a pale, pale man. As white as they come. Sickly, even. Combine this with my thick Homer Simpson beard that grows back the instant it is shaved, and you either have someone who should have starred in the sequel to *The Pianist* or at the very least someone who should never appear on TV without some sort of assistance from the good people at MAC.

Then, when I arrived at TSN, I suddenly had professionals to do my makeup for me. It was every boy's childhood dream! No longer would I have to worry about my container of foundation exploding in my pocket like a dropped bag of flour. Now I could just sit back, relax, and catch up on industry gossip. The makeup room is *always* the place to go for the latest chatter. People love to confess things to their makeup artists as if they were their therapists. If anyone should write a tell-all book about the history of Canadian television it should be someone who has done makeup in this industry for a few decades. The ladies of the makeup room basically run the network from within.

When I started at the network, the makeup artists were using a motorized spray machine to apply makeup, much like a pressure washer or a paint machine. They would pour liquid makeup foundation into a canister, hold the nozzle up to our faces, and paint them. Please, no porno jokes. This was a super-fast way of getting in and out of the makeup chair every night. I was perfectly happy to participate in the spray method for the rest of my days at TSN. That was, until a couple of years later when CTV abandoned the practice. Turns out all those fumes from the spray machine may have in fact been permeating the air in the makeup room and slowly killing us. It was kind of like when people first learned asbestos was bad for you after having spent their entire lives working in an asbestos factory. I look forward to suing CTV over the matter one day.

So now it's back to the old-fashioned way of having makeup applied: with sponges and powder puffs and brushes and, in the case of one veteran makeup artist, the occasional round of sexual harassment in the chair.

For years our regular nighttime makeup artist was a TV industry veteran named Elaine Saunders. *Mrs. Saunders*, as she would call herself, was a widow who had worked in Canadian television for around forty years and was finishing her work tenure at CTV with a cushy gig as *National News* anchor Lloyd Robertson's main makeup artist. Since Lloyd basically worked the same hours we did, Mrs. Saunders happily did our makeup as well. I became very fond of Mrs. Saunders, but she really was kind of crazy. I asked her if I could say that about her in this book and she said, "Yes, you idiot!" and then laughed. Mrs. Saunders grew up in the industry and worked on many of the most famous shows in Canadian television history. She spent decades at the CBC during the glory years, a time when many Canadians had only their public broadcaster to turn to for entertainment on the tube. She was there when working in Canadian television actually seemed to be a prestigious thing to do. But Mrs. Saunders wasn't living in the past. I think she enjoyed her CTV years almost as much as her CBC years because she had free rein to terrorize us in the makeup chair. She could also be wildly funny.

I loved to hear her tell stories about making up Scott Thompson and Bruce McCulloch in drag for *Kids in the Hall*, or taking the shine off Johnny Cash's forehead for his latest appearance on *The Tommy Hunter Show*. Mrs. Saunders probably made Johnny Cash up when he was addicted to painkillers and likely made up several booze and drug addicts in her television travels. She did work in television, after all.

She would also talk about her appreciation of the kindness of Vegas hookers ("They're so pretty and so sweet. I love when one or two of them get on the same elevator as me at the Bellagio!"), and the fact that she planned to move into my condo with me at any moment. "You'll just have to buy a condo big enough for my tchotchkes!" she'd insist. (I'm pretty sure tchotchkes are "old-lady knick-knacks," but you'd have to ask Mrs. Saunders to be sure.)

Mrs. Saunders was also Joan Rivers's personal makeup artist for the comedienne's regular monthly appearances on the Shopping Channel. She had known and worked with Joan for many years, and she and Joan had a love-hate relationship. Yet you have to admire Mrs. Saunders for doing makeup for a seventy-two-year-old woman whose face had been stretched to the point that her pores surely had the consistency of dried pavement. Making up Joan must have been like spreading flour on the sidewalk with a spatula.

I could always tell what kind of mood Joan had been in the previous weekend at the Shopping Channel by the way Mrs. Saunders acted on Monday after working with her. If she was bright and cheerful and showing off some brand of cheap earrings and bangles that Joan had given her, then it had been a positive work experience for Mrs. Saunders. If she was quiet and sullen and lamenting her lot in life, then Joan had been in a bad mood throughout her Shopping Channel duties. Mrs. Saunders called Joan Rivers by her real name, Mrs. Rosenberg, and Mrs. Rosenberg did a lot of nice things for Mrs. Saunders. By all accounts, Mrs. R was clearly a *very* generous person with people she cared about. I honestly think the two ladies saw a lot of themselves in each other: They were trailblazers in an industry that was once completely run by men.

Every night when I'd arrive at work I'd head straight to the makeup room, and the routine would always be the same. Mrs. Saunders would apply a layer of makeup to my beard and under my eyes, followed by a dash of powder to take away the shine and a quick comb of the bushiest eyebrows this side of Gene Shalit. Then she would ask me to feel her tits.

If there's such a thing as being sexually harassed in a humorous and relatively harmless way, then it happened to me in Mrs. Saunders's makeup chair. I don't mean to make light of sexual harassment. I'm well aware that it's a serious issue in many a workplace. My situation was slightly different, however. We're talking about a woman, nearing her seventies, who was having a little fun at my expense. This has not scarred me. I would never sue Mrs. Saunders for sexual harassment. If there is a way I can sue CTV for it in the future, then of course I will. At this point I think it pretty much goes without saying that my "retirement plan" is to sue CTV at some point in the future for some sort of made-up trauma. It really does make more sense than RRSPs.

Mrs. Saunders's regular wardrobe would usually consist of some sort of bedazzled sweater or sweatshirt that she could easily lift up. This is something she would do very near my face about once a week. She would stand right beside me as I sat in her makeup chair, then she would begin with what I can only imagine was her idea of "setting the mood."

"What do you think about old people having sex?" she would begin with a wry smile.

"Mrs. Saunders, do we have to go through this every single night?" I'd reply.

"Old wrinkly bodies, farting, burping, bumping together, and having sex. Their undergarments smelling like pee . . ." Mrs. Saunders really should have written for Penthouse Forum.

Mrs. Saunders had been widowed several years earlier, and whenever I broached the subject of her dating again she would practically gag. "Old men are burping, farting dogs," she'd reply. "I don't want to have to deal with that every night. I already did it." Then upon realizing she had been distracted from her present task of getting me to touch her boobs, she'd fire up the "dirty talk" again, not realizing or caring that she was contradicting what she had just said. "Just imagine two old people getting down and dirty between the sheets! Plump old bodies banging together, sweating! So hot!"

"Mrs. Saunders, I *really* don't want to think about that," I'd plead to no avail.

I know what you're thinking: "Onrait, you've just never had to deal with a woman who is going through menopause." Sorry, my well-educated friends. This woman was beyond menopause. This was a woman who simply loved to *fuck with people's minds*. Sitting in her makeup chair every night was like signing up for it. After a few more minutes of dirty talk, Mrs. Saunders would lift up her bedazzled sweatshirt. Underneath this sparkly shirt, to my horror, she would be wearing an "old woman bra." This "bra" looked suspiciously like a full-body bandage that a young doctor would have used to patch up a wounded soldier in Vietnam. It supported not only her "droopy tits" (again, her words) but basically her entire torso as well. It was a little like one imagines Mormon undergarments to be. She would proudly stick her chest out like a peacock.

"Feel my tits!" she'd demand with a grin, making it sound like this should be a privilege for me. She was not asking.

"Mrs. Saunders! I'm not going to feel your tits!"

"Don't you wanna feel my tits?" She'd be stifling a giggle at this point.

"No, Mrs. Saunders, I *do not* want to grab your jugs."

"Why not? Don't you think I'm sexy?"

"I just don't think of you in that way, Mrs. Saunders."

"Why not?"

"I guess for starters I would answer by saying that you're old enough to be my grandmother."

"I've got experience!"

"You *do* realize that this is sexual harassment, don't you?"

"What's that?" she'd ask innocently.

"If I were to report you to human resources you could be fired! Do you want that?"

"Oh, I don't fucking care!" Mrs. Saunders would happily reply. "What the hell are they going to do to me now?" She really did have a point.

Eventually she'd pull the shirt down, sufficiently happy that she'd humiliated and embarrassed me to her satisfaction. Then she'd throw a little more makeup on my giant forehead, helping to keep the shine from blinding people, and send me on my way.

Half the time all I could think about was *Did Mrs. Saunders flash her tits at Johnny Cash like this?* The Man in Black probably loved every second of it, though Mrs. Saunders was a bit younger then. And what about Tommy Hunter himself? The ol' Canadian country crooner is famously a man of the Lord. Surely he did not take kindly to his makeup artist telling him to pluck her nipples like guitar strings?

This behaviour continued regularly until she retired in 2011. I pretty much got used to it, and it always made me laugh. CTV News Channel prime-time anchor Marcia MacMillan walked in on Mrs. S yanking up the bedazzled sweater more than once and shielded her eyes as if she'd just witnessed a horrific accident. For almost ten years Mrs. Saunders was a constant, sexually harassing companion at work, and dealing with her became as much a part of my routine as reading the teleprompter.

I was sad to see Mrs. Saunders retire but at the same time happy I would no longer be subjected to the daily sight of her entire naked torso wrapped in swaddling clothes shoved inches from my cheek. She told me she plans to become a part-time "slot slut" at the casino (her words), where she'll probably befriend more hookers and likely become the world's oldest and most successful pimp. She also said she plans to do part-time makeup work on the side, which should serve as a warning to all future broadcasters. I really will miss seeing her every day. Please don't tell her this or she'll show up at my door at some point wearing nothing but a potato sack and holding a stack of boxes.

"The rest of the tchotchkes are in the car," she'll say.

CHAPTER 23

The Olympics! On CTV!

ORIGINALLY, I WAS KIND OF an afterthought when it came to the Vancouver Olympic Games coverage. I was just happy to have been asked to go at all because not everyone at TSN was so lucky. My original assignment was to simply keep doing what I did every night: host the 10:00 PT edition of *SportsCentre* on TSN. Dan and I were asked to host together, and to be honest we were really excited about the proposition. We knew it was a job we could do in our sleep and wouldn't involve much preparation. We could show up, write and host the show, and then head out to the Roxy every night for drinks with the crew. The Olympics! On TSN!

About three months before the Games were scheduled to start, I got a phone call from Rick Chisholm, the former head of production at TSN who was now serving as head of production for the Olympic Consortium. He explained that they were trying to formulate a plan for coverage of the Games on CTV in the early morning. I had assumed that *Canada AM* would simply continue to do what they were doing in that slot, and maybe even expand from three hours to six. I think there may have been some concern that without actual sports broadcasters on the show, the morning coverage might dissolve into chaos. It dissolved into chaos all right, but I ended up being the one leading the charge.

Rick said he wanted to change my Olympic assignment and that now I would host a new show, called *Olympic Morning* on CTV during the Games. I was told I would be co-anchoring with *Canada AM* host Beverly Thomson in Vancouver, while Bev's regular co-host on *AM*, Seamus O'Reagan, would be hosting with *CP24 Breakfast* host Melissa Grelo in Whistler. If that sounded confusing, trust me, we were just getting started. But I made the incorrect assumption that there was a big, grand plan for the show already in place and this entire proposition had been well thought out.

Don't get me wrong. I was genuinely excited about the idea that Rick had apparently hand-picked me to anchor this new show, but I was already a bit concerned after asking him a few questions. Questions as simple as "What time will the show be on?"

"You'll start at 3:00 a.m. local time and finish up at 9:00 a.m.!" answered Rick cheerfully, trying to sound as enthusiastic as possible.

"I'm sorry?"

"Hey, I didn't say it was going to be *easy*."

I did a quick bit of math in my head and realized that in order to prepare and write for the show, I would have to be in the studio at midnight every day at the *latest*. The show would run throughout the Olympics, so that meant seventeen days of starting at midnight and finishing at 9:00 a.m., not counting a post-show debrief that may take an hour or two. For the privilege of moving from a TSN program to a CTV one, I was going from working a one-hour show to a six-hour show. This didn't do anything to dampen my enthusiasm, however; I was aware this was a more high-profile gig and ultimately a positive move for me. But as I pressed on with questions for Rick, I began to wonder what I had signed on for.

"How will we fill the show's content between the hours of 3:00 a.m. and, say, 7:00 a.m., before any of the athletes are up and no events are being held?" I wondered aloud.

Rick's answer: "We've talked about maybe setting up a camera in the Olympic Village and doing interviews with the athletes that way."

Was this a joke? Did they really think that Olympic athletes who had trained for this moment for four long years would be interested in waking up in the middle of the night and breaking their routines so we could do a four-minute interview? I was beginning to worry, but Rick assured me everything would be taken care of.

I arrived a day before the Games began, and we were off.

People have often commented that Beverly didn't seem to "warm up" to me until about Day 3 of the Games, and I suppose that's probably true. I actually thought we got along really well right away, and I did my very best to include her in everything I did. Perhaps Bev was as frustrated with the entire process for the first couple of days as I was and decided by the third day there was nothing she could do about it, and it was best to just roll with the punches. Or perhaps it just took her a while to get used to my crap. Either way, I can think of *several* other anchors whom I had less chemistry with than Bev Thomson. I found her to be a really wonderful person behind the scenes as well. She had beaten cancer, had recently divorced, and was raising two children in Toronto essentially on her own. Yet she was pretty much eternally upbeat and truly the voice of sanity for me at the Games. I honestly don't know what I would've done had she not been there with me.

The show featured an entire cast of characters: I mentioned the four hosts including me, then there were Dan and Jessi from *The Hills After Show* on MTV; Elaine "Lainey" Lui was our Olympic gossip correspondent; and *Canada AM* weatherman Jeff Hutcheson was out in a remote location, usually Robson Square. Gino Reda, my TSN cohort, was also on board to serve as our hockey analyst. Gino also proved to be a voice of sanity in a sea of production chaos. He worked tirelessly at the Games, going to all of Team Canada's practices and hosting an Olympic Web hockey show at night, then stumbling into the studio, sometimes with no sleep at all, and appearing with me for a few segments. Gino also proved to be a wonderful guest booker as well, even though that was absolutely not in his job description. He brought Wayne Gretzky and Mark Messier in to the studio at an ungodly hour; they both happily obliged because, well, you just don't say no to Gino.

At one point, about halfway through the Games, with fatigue and delusion setting in, we were in the middle of a commercial break when Jen, our producer, informed us we would be coming back from the commercial break on-camera and throwing it to a live shot of a café on Robson Street, where revellers were still up partying from the night before. Remember, our show started at 3:00 a.m. local time, so pretty much every night when I walked to the studio around midnight, I would pass pack after pack of drunks. Or, on one fateful rainy night, my colleague Dave Randorf and his girlfriend walking hand-in-hand like two teenage lovers. I hated them. I hated all of them for being off when I had to work. (How quickly I had forgotten the advice the Edmonton camera guy had given me all those years ago: *You will always be working when everyone else is off.*)

So Bev and I were supposed to send it down to the drunks on Robson, which we had done a few times already on our show during the Games to varying degrees of success. And by "varying degrees of success," I mean in general it was usually a complete shit show. I'd made the assumption that it was poor Jeff Hutcheson who'd been told to round up the drunks and interview them and that we would be throwing to him, but instead Producer Jen said: "Send it down to a café on Robson Street and throw it to Rena. She's the one interviewing the inebriated."

I looked at Bev for a moment. Then I hit the talkback button that allowed me to speak directly to Jen.

"Uh, Jen?" I asked.

"Yes?"

"Who the fuck is Rena?"

Turns out no one had bothered to tell us that CTV had flown out another on-air personality named Rena Heer from CP24 to serve as an extra remote host. It is the first and only time I have participated in a broadcast where I didn't know who all my fellow hosts were.

We were usually able to drag one or more of our Olympic analysts into the studio to fill a segment or two. One night I was sprinting through the International Broadcast Centre in hot pursuit of an Olympic muffin for me and an Olympic yogurt for Bev. Suddenly, out of the corner of my eye I spotted an older gentleman wearing what is widely known as a "Canadian tuxedo": denim shirt and denim trousers. I believe he may even have been wearing a denim hat. I looked closer and realized it was in fact none other than CTV's *Olympic Prime Time* host Brian Williams, the veteran of twelve Olympics, which he had mentioned to me at least twelve times. I found Brian to be quirky, charming, and completely supportive of everything I did.

Every time I run into Brian he tells me the same story: Back when he was working for the CBC and Ralph Mellanby was producing *Hockey Night in Canada*, Ralph would apparently tell Brian that his unique style of broadcasting was his calling card and that he should never change. Brian always told me that he thinks of this whenever he watches me, which I find incredibly flattering. I can say that Brian has never been anything less than incredibly supportive about me and my career, and we have a really great relationship.

I wasn't sure why the hell Brian was there at 3:30 in the morning, since his *Prime Time* show had ended at 11:00 and he probably should have been asleep. I noticed he was frantically searching around on a desk for something.

"Brian! What are you doing here?" I called out. He turned around and saw me.

"Hey, Jay! I'm here looking for my notebook. I've lost my notebook with all my research and information about the Games, and I need it for my next broadcast. I've got to have that notebook."

I instantly felt terrible for Brian since I knew he was as much a creature of habit as I was. This was probably killing him.

"Brian, I'm so sorry," I answered back. "But listen, since you're here anyway, why don't you come on the show for a segment? It will only be four minutes. We can talk about the Games so far and how you think Canadians are faring. We can even talk about your notebook. Maybe someone out there has it and will return it! What do you say? Come on the show for a few minutes?"

Brian took one quick look at me and said, "Jay, don't be a smartass."

Not sure if he ever found that notebook.

Each day blurred into the next. I realized this is what it must be like to have to actually work for a living.

By week two, some CTV personalities had started to voice concerns that they weren't being utilized enough during the Games coverage. And by "not enough" I mean "not at all." CTV's solution was to have them come on our show. One segment featured Tanya Kim from *etalk*, Leah Miller from *So You Think You Can Dance Canada*, and Jeanne Beker from *Fashion Television*. Tanya and Leah were both incredibly nice, and Jeanne was a true professional who had a great attitude even though she admitted she didn't even understand why she was there. Especially since she was supposed to be at New York Fashion Week at this point in time. Imagine if the Super Bowl was going on and someone said to an NFL football analyst who had been covering the league for the entire season, "We're

Jay Onrait

not going to send you to the Super Bowl. We want all our talent at the Olympics."

"But what am I going to do there?" the talent might ask.

"We'll figure it out when we get there" would be the reply. That should be the motto of Canadian broadcast television: *We'll Figure It Out When We Get There.*

Jeanne could have sulked and complained about the fact that she was forced to miss out on the most important event of her journalistic calendar. Instead, she came in every day with a smile and had nothing but nice things to say to me and everyone on the crew. She was paired with two girls who were almost young enough to be her daughters but didn't question it, at least not to me. She allowed the other girls to take the lead while she quietly sat and waited to make her points. Seeing someone with her experience and talent handle the situation that way made me pull up my own boot-straps, stop complaining so much, and buckle down a bit. The girls would come on the show each morning during the final hour from 8:00 a.m. to 9:00 a.m. local time, an hour I quickly coined "the CTV Olympic Galaxy of Stars Hour."

One day after discussing the ridiculously long lineup at The Bay's Olympic store (literally down the block; I couldn't believe it), the girls announced they had brought a present for me: a pair of Canadian Olympic–themed boxer shorts. I was thrilled to receive the gag gift, even though I was well aware that, being a man, I would actually *wear* these boxer shorts on a regular basis when the Games were over because I am cheap. Give a man a pair of free underwear and he will most likely wear that underwear.

After the segment with Leah, Tanya, and Jeanne was over, the girls were whisked away and I had a two-minute commercial break to prepare for the next segment. J.D., the floor director, mentioned that I should put the shorts on and model them on-air. At that point, I had already brought an Olympic rubber chicken mascot on-air, an

Olympic banana, and Olympic mittens, so it stood to reason that the Olympic boxers should get equal airtime. But I was skeptical. I thought maybe the higher-ups would think it was too much and perhaps I'd get in trouble for it. They weren't exactly thrilled about the Olympic chicken. But J.D. was insistent, almost like a drill sergeant:

"Strip. Put 'em on," he said sternly.

Thirty seconds left in the commercial break.

"I don't know, man," I said sheepishly.

Fifteen seconds.

"Do it!" he said with a grin. Watching me humiliate myself was keeping the crew sane.

I decided I couldn't say no to J.D., and I dropped my pants in front of the entire crew and our remaining guests, including Susanne Boyce, who at the time was essentially running the CTV Television Network. Luckily I wasn't going commando that day, and I decided it would be for the best if I didn't take off the boxer briefs I currently had on. I wanted to push the envelope, but I didn't want to get arrested. I pulled the shorts on over the briefs a mere two seconds before we returned live to the nation. Sitting alongside Bev as we closed the show for the day, I caught a shot of myself in our studio monitor. Brown socks, brown dress shoes, suit jacket, shirt, tie, and no pants. Nether regions covered by a pair of Olympic boxer shorts. The boxer shorts were bright white, and yet my pale legs outshone them.

"Look at *those* pearly whites," I said.

The show became more and more popular. We even somehow managed to convince Jimmy Fallon to come on while he was in town taping some bit for his new NBC late-night show. Much taller than you would expect, almost as tall as me, Jimmy took the time to take pictures with everyone who asked him, answering every request for a photo or autograph with a cheery "No problem, buddy!" His "handlers" waited impatiently on the sidelines as we whisked Jimmy into one of our Barcelona chairs. I needed something, anything, to make the interview just a little bit different from the standard interview Jimmy would have done with a local morning show in Ithaca, New York. No offense to the good people of Ithaca, New York, but I needed something that Jimmy and I could perhaps have a little comic moment with.

Our crew had spent the previous two weeks complaining about the number of hours they were working compared with what they were being paid, leading to the inspiration for my Jimmy Fallon comedy prop. I asked around to the crew, and one of our lighting guys reached into his wallet and had exactly what I needed.

As the interview ended I said to Jimmy, "I just wanted to give you a gift before you go. You see, Jimmy, we've been working so hard here at the Olympics, and our compensation hasn't been great."

"Oh, yeah?" said Jimmy, confused and likely a little scared.

"In fact, I'm going to sacrifice my day's compensation so you can see what it's like to work for a Canadian television network. Here you go, Sir."

I handed him a few wadded bills of Canadian Tire money.

After the final *Olympic Morning* ended with a staged bit where I was officially "fired" from CTV and arrested by two International Broadcast Centre security guards while Bev packed up her carry-on luggage and wheeled it off-set, I was completely exhausted and ready to sleep for four weeks. However, there was one major event still to come that would close out the Games: the men's hockey final between Canada and the USA.

CHAPTER 24

Run, Onrait, Run

SOMETIMES PEOPLE ASK ME if I have access to every sporting event on the planet, and the answer is absolutely not. I can sneak my way into the press box for almost any pro sports game in North America, but the Olympics were a whole other animal. For obvious reasons security was way more intense, though while I was in a media line to get into a preliminary-round men's hockey game between Canada and Switzerland, I saw Brendan Shanahan sneak Jason Bateman and Will Arnett past the line and into the building. *What if Shanny were a terrorist?* I wondered to myself.

After the final *Olympic Morning* was over and we'd said our goodbyes, I went back to my room to change and grab a quick bite of room service. The plan was to meet up with my *Olympic Morning* director, Nilesh Hathi, and his wife, Liz, who had also worked on our show. The three of us planned to watch the gold-medal game at the Molson Canadian Hockey House, essentially a beer tent with over-priced Molson beers and live bands where you could watch all the hockey games. It seemed as good a place to go as any. I had tried to get a pass into the press box, but they were understandably hard to come by at that point, and I couldn't argue that I was "covering the game" since my Olympic responsibilities had ended that morning.

Nilesh and Liz stopped by my hotel to pick me up about two hours later, and we started walking toward the beer tent. About ten steps into our walk they broke the news: They had somehow managed to secure two tickets to the game from an international media member whom Nilesh had worked with at one point in his career. Never had the phrase "Be nice to everyone you work with" rung more true than that day. Nilesh and Liz tried their best to downplay their good fortune, but there was no hiding it: I was being deservedly ditched and now had no one to watch the gold-medal game with. I considered heading back to my hotel room and watching the game alone, but that seemed downright pathetic. Even stumbling into the most crowded and disgusting downtown Vancouver pub by myself seemed like a better option than that. Instead I continued to walk to MCHH, figuring I would surely see someone down there that I knew.

The walk took about half an hour, and by the time I arrived there was already a massive lineup at Hockey House. David Kines, the former VP of programming at MuchMusic, had told me I could come in the VIP entrance. I was about to head in when I checked my phone and saw I had received a message from Susanne Boyce, then head of programming for CTV:

"Where are you?"

Curious, I replied back instantly: "I'm down at Molson Canadian Hockey House."

A few seconds later, a reply from Susanne: "Oh, too bad. I have a ticket to the gold-medal game."

Sweet Lord.

A shot of adrenaline ran through my body. My fingers were shaking as I typed:

"You hold on to that ticket. I will be RIGHT THERE."

"Ok, haha," she replied.

It was just thirty minutes to puck drop.

The next fifteen minutes of my life could best be described as the final scene from *Ferris Bueller's Day Off* with Ferris running through the streets and backyards of his Chicago suburb in order to beat his parents home and keep them from discovering he skipped school. Cabs were not an option. There was no way of hailing one back to the International Broadcast Centre where Susanne was; the streets were packed with people, and cabs were nowhere to be found. Transit was an even worse idea. Certainly, no buses were getting around downtown that day. There was simply no other option: *Run, Onrait, run.*

If you're not familiar with downtown Vancouver, I can safely say that not only did I have a big run ahead of me but I had a big *uphill* run ahead of me. The Molson Canadian Hockey House was steps from Canada Hockey Place, aka GM Place, later to be renamed Rogers Arena, but forever known as the rink where the Canucks play. Susanne and the precious golden ticket were back at the International Broadcast Centre where we broadcast *Olympic Morning* and all the other shows, otherwise known as Canada Place and also the former Canadian pavilion at Expo 86. The distance wasn't so much an issue; despite my poor conditioning, I should still have been able to make it there and back with ease. But there was one problem: The first half of the run was essentially *all uphill*.

I could hear the song that played at the end of *Ferris Bueller* in my head as I sprinted through the streets of Vancouver past red mittens and toques and signs and Canadian flags and so many happy people, so many smiles. I was trying to focus on the task at hand: If I could make it there and back in half an hour, I wouldn't miss the drop of the puck. There was something else motivating me: Susanne was one of *the* bigwigs at CTV. This "golden ticket" she had for me surely would not be in the nosebleed section. There was a chance I could have one of the best seats in the house for one of the most important hockey games in Canadian history. *Run, Onrait, run!*

Like anyone in my situation, I was fuelled by adrenaline at the beginning of the run. I was making excellent time as I navigated my way uphill. I was acquainted enough with my surroundings that I didn't make any wrong turns, but about halfway through my journey I started to really slow down. I am a skinny man who is blessed with great metabolism for my age, but this should not be mistaken for excellent conditioning. The most exercise I usually get is a bike ride to the Drake Hotel café in downtown Toronto for eggs Benedict, a *very leisurely* bike ride, I might add. Not to mention I didn't exactly spend my customary twenty minutes stretching. I started to cramp up in my stomach, my legs were giving out, and I was sweating like Patrick Ewing in the 1994 NBA Finals. Scratch that: I was sweating like Ted Striker at the end of *Airplane!* ("The gear is down, and we're ready to land!") I could barely see through the sweat dripping down my ragged face, but the idea of clutching that golden ticket kept me moving until I finally arrived at the IBC, only halfway through my journey. I sprinted up the escalator to the CTV Olympic studios, frantically calling out to anyone, *everyone*, that I recognized, "HAS ANYONE SEEN SUSANNE? HAS ANYONE SEEN SUSANNE?" In my sweaty and frantic condition, people must have wondered if I had come to kill her.

Finally, I spotted Susanne casually speaking with a group of executives as if she wasn't holding a ticket that was likely worth $5,000 at that point. She spotted me out of the corner of her eye, smiled, reached into a bag over her shoulder, lifted the ticket out, and held it up like it was Simba at the beginning of *The Lion King*.

"Looking for this?" she asked.

"Man, am I glad to see you!" I proclaimed, completely aware

that I really had no time for small talk with this woman, even though I still had to display how gracious and appreciative I was to receive the ticket.

"I have a favour to ask you," she said calmly. She was kindly ignoring the fact that sweat was dripping on my shoes.

Oh, Christ, I thought, *am I going to have to perform sexual favours on this woman to get this ticket?* I quickly surmised that I would, in fact, perform sexual favours on this woman to secure this ticket. I didn't even hesitate for a second. This was, after all, Team Canada in a gold-medal Olympic hockey game. I would very likely have agreed to sexual favours if Susanne had been a man. Turns out that wasn't what she was looking for.

"You're going to be sitting next to Craig Kielburger. You know who that is, right?"

"Of course," I lied.

"You're going to be sitting next to him at the game. I need you to entertain him. Make sure he has a good time."

So many things went through my head at that moment: *Make sure he has a good time? At the gold-medal men's hockey game at the Olympics?* If this man needed me to make sure he had a good time at this event, he needed to hand in his passport. Nonetheless, I agreed to the request without hesitation, snatched the ticket from her hand, thanked her profusely, and began the run back to the arena. The good news is that the run was now mostly downhill toward the water. The bad news is that I was physically exhausted and very likely in the worst shape of anyone in the city of Vancouver at the time. I refused to miss puck drop, however, and I still had fifteen minutes. It would be just enough. I navigated the streets of Vancouver past hordes of excited Canadian hockey fans heading to their designated spots to catch the game, many of them calling my name. "ONRAIT, WHERE YA GOING?"

"Can't . . . [gasp] . . . talk . . . [wheeze] now . . ." I'd reply with a smile. It was kind of fun. Kind of. I hoped I didn't die on the way to the most important sporting event I would ever attend in my life. That would really be tragic. Sort of fitting for a sportscaster I suppose, but tragic. But I didn't die on the run to the arena. I made it with minutes to spare. As I made my way further and further down the lower bowl, I realized that the entire Olympic experience had been worth it: I suddenly found myself five rows up from centre ice, about five rows in front of Mr. William Shatner, and I took my seat right next to Craig Kielburger. I later discovered that Mr. Kielburger was the co-founder, along with his brother Marc, of Free the Children, a children's rights advocacy group. At the time he was just twenty-seven years old and had already been awarded the Order of Canada. Craig had recently returned from Haiti, where the tragic 2010 earthquake had just taken place. He was genuinely nice, great to talk to, and took none of my energy.

The Golden Goal was as great as I'd imagined it would be in my head, and I realized the very moment Sidney Crosby scored that I was probably the luckiest man in the world.

CHAPTER 25

The Week That Wasn't

I JUST WANTED TO DO a simple little show. Nothing special. Something I could do on the side while I continued my duties at TSN. It had been over a year since I'd hosted *Olympic Morning* and very little had come of it. I had been heaped with praise but it had resulted in nothing further. I did get *one* offer. Nan Row, executive producer of *The Marilyn Denis Show*, kindly offered to make me a regular contributor as the "dating expert" from a male perspective. While I appreciated the opportunity, I didn't exactly think that was in my wheelhouse. Not to mention I had just started a relationship and my entire presence on that show would have been an elaborate lie. Not that television is slim on elaborate lies. We once convinced ourselves it was a good idea to have puppets in the intermission of hockey games at TSN.

I had always been a fan of *The Soup* with Joel McHale on E! network. When the show started back in 2003, my then wife and I would watch it all the time. I loved the concept of the show. It was formerly known as *Talk Soup*, a clip show specifically focusing on chat shows and especially the chat shows of the 1990s. Trashy shows that were hot at the time, like the ones with Morton Downey Jr., Ricki Lake, and Jerry Springer. The show was hosted by a rotation of heavily talented actors and comedians starting with Greg Kinnear and followed up by John Henson, Hal Sparks, and Aisha Tyler. Once reality shows started to take over the television landscape, E! decided to rebrand it as *The Soup* and hired McHale, a comedian and actor from Seattle, to be the new host. McHale was great on the show, but the clips were the real star. Soon there were regular categories of clips like "What the Kids Are Watching," "Reality Show Clip Time!" and "Chat Stew," the latter focusing on those chat show clips that were once the sole focus on the show and were now simply part of a bigger entity. It wasn't a huge hit, but it was a cult hit, the best kind of hit.

It wasn't long into *The Soup*'s run that I began to wonder if this was a concept that might work in Canada. Even back in 2003, Canadian reality shows were being produced in mass quantity. *Canadian Idol* was doing exceptionally well for CTV, not to mention a gaggle of homemade reality shows and cooking shows on HGTV and Food Network Canada like *Holmes on Homes*, *Canada's Worst Driver*, and *Canada's Worst Handyman*. Then there was "Coach's Corner" on *Hockey Night in Canada*, as well as *Canada AM* and *George Stroumboulopoulos Tonight*, plus all the great local news clips from all the Canadian networks. So many funny moments were happening on these shows, some intentionally, most unintentionally. It was time to celebrate our own television mishaps! I figured if they could do *The Soup* in the States, why couldn't we do it here?

The concept stayed in my brain for years as I rose through the ranks at TSN and focused on my career at hand. There wasn't really a lot of time to pitch a new television show. Oh, who am I kidding? I was just extremely lazy. Finally, in the late spring of 2011, upon coming to the realization that no one was going to approach me from CTV, I decided to get off my lazy ass and do something about it.

One of my *Olympic Morning* producers was Mark McInnis, who at the time was also head of programming for MTV Canada. Mark was the kind of person that I instantly bonded with. A gentle and genuinely creative soul, he was extremely encouraging and didn't have the bitter edge that so many TV execs in this country seem to have acquired over too many years of working in this business.

Mark was in charge of MTV's highly successful *The Hills After Show*, and he was the first person I thought of when considering a Canadian version of *The Soup*. At the very least, I thought Mark could steer me in the right direction of people who might be able to get the show off the ground. He was very close with Susanne Boyce, who had recently left the company after being CTV's head of programming for several years. So, the person who essentially brought Mark into the fold had *just left the company*. This probably should have been an indication to me that Mark might not be long for the company either, but I was too worried about making sure my pitch was right instead of figuring out the right person to pitch to. Remember: *not much of a details guy.*

I told Mark my plan: The country had been producing so much original reality and news programming in the past ten years that it was time for a Canadian version of *The Soup* to celebrate all of it. I told Mark I knew it would be tricky: Networks like Global and CBC probably wouldn't be eager to let us use clips of their shows and make fun of their talent, but I said that I thought we could be patient and wait them out. CBC might be been a government-funded network, but they needed to promote their shows as much as anyone did. If they allowed us to use a funny clip of a retired hockey player competing on *Battle of the Blades*, we could offer some free promotion for that show in exchange, perhaps introduce a newer, younger, hipper audience to a show like that. But that was a big *if*. There was a chance Global and Citytv could hold out for years before letting us use clips from their shows, if they let us use them at all.

The good news, I reasoned, was that CTV now owned so many different networks that we probably had enough material for a show within the walls of our own company. Between shows like *MTV Live* and *1 Girl 5 Gays* on MTV Canada, and *New.Music.Live.* on MuchMusic, and *Canada's Worst Driver* on the Discovery Channel, and *Stratusphere* on Travel and Escape, and all the shows on CTV, like *etalk*, well, it's safe to say we thought we had the content to at least do a half-hour a week. Any concern about the show looking like a promo clip for CTV network was certainly justified, but if the show was funny enough, I reasoned, other networks would come calling. Surely Citytv wouldn't be too protective of a show like *Canada Sings!* in which they themselves were making fun of bad contestants. There was also plenty of online content being produced in this country as well, enough for a few clips a week for sure.

Mark loved the idea of the show and quickly brought in his senior creative producer, Ben Rotterman, to help shepherd it along. I told both gentlemen it might be a good idea for us to actually approach the producers of *The Soup* about using their show title graphics, music, and even a copy of their "set." There was already a *Canadian Idol*, a *Canada's Got Talent*, a *So You Think You Can Dance Canada*. It wasn't as if we would be breaking the mould by producing *The Canadian Soup*. If anything, I thought it would lend legitimacy to the show.

But Mark and Ben didn't like the idea of doing a Canadian version of *The Soup*. In their minds it made more sense to call the show something completely different and make it our own right from the start. There was a method to their madness: The two of them were essentially in control of programming at MTV, MuchMore, and MuchMusic, and they reasoned that by starting the show on one of those networks and calling it something new and unique, we would have some ownership over it and hopefully it would be given a longer time to find its way and be successful. I had seen shows like *Late Night with Jimmy Fallon* start out slowly. Had NBC given Jimmy only a month or two, the show would likely have gone down as a miserable failure. Same with *Seinfeld*. Same with *Beverly Hills, 90210*. I reasoned that if we could make the show a hit on a network like MTV or MuchMore, then a spot would be found for us on the main network. Or not. I didn't really care. I just wanted to do a simple little television show that I would be proud of week after week. I wasn't really concerned about *where* it aired. I just wanted it *on* the air.

This may be a point where a reasonable person would say, "Shouldn't you have a manager or agent negotiate these things for you? Aren't you a creative type who should just be worried about content?" When Mark and Ben agreed to shoot a pilot for the show, I was just happy to be *doing something* within the CTV family for the first time since the Olympics. My basic philosophy was: Get the show on the air and make sure it's good, and the rest will take care of itself. I didn't care about money. This was about doing something I loved and truly cared about.

I was assigned a show producer named Michael MacKinnon, who had started out in the business shooting and editing *The Buzz*, a comedy show that started on Rogers Cable TV and eventually made its way onto the Comedy Network. *The Buzz* starred Daryn Jones and Mistah Mo and was almost a precursor to *Punk'd*, *Jackass*, and shows like that. I always thought Daryn was a really funny and talented guy and was surprised it took so long for him to find a home on conventional television, co-hosting MTV Live and working for Mark McInnis and then eventually moving to the CBC. Michael was also a funny and talented guy, and he was genuinely enthusiastic about the project. So we had Mike on board, and Ben and Mark were on board; it was time to shoot a pilot for the show. We wanted to stick to material we knew we had access to rather than trying to do a pilot that featured a bunch of clips we couldn't use anyway. For the most part we stuck to Internet clips and a ton of MTV Canada and MuchMusic-based clips, knowing we had access to all of them and would probably be using a ton of that material going forward.

After Michael and his crew assembled enough clips for a credible pilot, the two of us sat down and wrote some intros and jokes for the clips—nothing too hilarious, just funny enough to give senior CTV execs an idea of the tone. The whole thing made me feel really happy, like I was finally accomplishing something outside of TSN. We were shooting a pilot for a real TV show. In Canada! It was practically a miracle.

Mike, Mark, and Ben came up with the name *The Week That Was*. I didn't love the title. I felt it had been used on a bunch of radio and television shows before and wasn't really unique enough. Again, though, I wasn't about to let a little detail like that derail our progress. We shot the pilot at the famous Masonic Temple in downtown Toronto, which was being used as a studio by CTV, mostly for MTV Canada, and has since been sold, likely to condo developers. The Temple had hosted a number of legendary bands on its mainstage over the years, even Led Zeppelin. I'd seen Sloan play there back in my Ryerson days. Our studio wasn't exactly a walk-in closet, but it was pretty close. It was about the size of a decent one-bedroom apartment. It really didn't matter because it was all we needed.

The pilot went as well as hoped: not mean-spirited, but rather a celebration of all the television being produced in this country. I had visions of *The Week That Was* being sold all over the world, with various foreign networks playing it for audiences who would laugh endlessly at Canadian TV clips. I was dreaming big. I didn't think it was the funniest show we could do, but I thought it conveyed the spirit of the show very well. I was confident we'd get picked up. And we did!

But it was complicated. My bosses at TSN had been *very* good about letting me shoot the pilot in the first place. They knew I wanted to try something new and were completely in favour of it as long as it didn't affect what I was doing at TSN day to day. That was the plan, anyway. Spend maybe three days a week working on *The Week That Was*: two days of writing and prep work, possibly pretaping one item per show, a comedy sketch or an interview perhaps, then on day three shoot the actual show and look ahead to next week. Keep in mind I was already working a full-time job. I didn't want the new show to take anything away from *SportsCentre*.

It didn't take long for the feedback on the new pilot to start coming back, and it was generally very positive. Apparently, the pilot was shown to the CTV sales team and was met with great enthusiasm, with several young salespeople, guys who had watched me for years on TSN, offering to sell the project to advertisers. Rick Brace, who was in charge of all CTV Specialty channels but had once been the president of TSN and was aware of my existence, gave the green light to the project. Rick was apparently concerned about our ability to secure clips for the new show, but Mark and Ben reassured him that there was enough content within the walls of CTV to get us started and we'd work from there. We were a go.

We had been promised only a limited early run, and it was my fault: I had to make my annual trek with Dan across the country to do live shows for the Kraft Celebration Tour in August, so *The Week That Was* would have to go on hiatus about four episodes in. Should we wait and launch the show after the Kraft Tour was over? Or produce and air four episodes during the summer, get our feet wet, and then return as a well-oiled machine after a two-week break? We were all eager to get going, so we decided to launch the show as soon as possible.

I had become acquainted with the Toronto-based Sketchersons comedy troupe through their weekly show, "Sunday Night Live" at the Comedy Bar in the Bloorcourt Village neighbourhood. I was actually honoured to have been asked to host the show, essentially a note-for-note live rendition of Saturday Night Live, complete with "Weekend Update" and a musical guest. The Sketchersons would frequently ask Toronto "celebrities" to host, like Mayor David Miller and former *Kids in the Hall* star Scott Thompson, as well as other local stand-up comedians and sketch comedians. I was asked to host the show in 2010 just after the Olympics, and I had a great time doing it.

I found everyone in the cast to be supremely talented and fun, and in particular I hit it off with a baseball- and *Battlestar Galactica*–loving nerd like me named Brendan Halloran. When it came time to find a writer for the show, I knew Brendan would be a great fit. He understood exactly what we were going for, but going in he was already understandably frustrated by the limitations of writing on our show. There was simply no way for us to be as mean-spiritedly funny as *The Soup* because we wanted to encourage other shows to sign up and let us use their clips. Still, I kept reminding Brendan that we had plenty of amazing footage that would make the show a definite hit. Or, if not a hit, at least a serviceable choice on Sunday afternoons while you're nursing a hangover.

We also hired two local stand-up comedians, Hunter Collins and Dini Dimakos, to gather our Canadian TV clips, and two up-and-coming young producers, Dave Grunier and Kate Morawetz, to handle the day-to-day production. We finished off our crew with Marla Black, who was responsible for "clearing clips," shorthand for "begging TV networks to let us use funny clips from their shows." In other words, she was the lynchpin for the entire operation. If Marla was unable to convince networks like Global to eventually let us use clips from *Recipe to Riches* on the Food Network, then in the long run the show really would look like a half-hour advertisement for CTV programming. No time to worry about the long run, though: We had two weeks of rehearsals before our first set of four shows. All I was worried about was making sure the show was *funny*.

The first week of rehearsal went well. We had some kinks to work out, but all in all I loved the content we had to work with. But four days before we were set to tape our first real show, things began to fall apart, and it was an innocent comment from Marla that made me realize how much trouble I was in, and how pitching the show had been a horrible mistake.

CHAPTER 26

What Do You Mean, We Can't

Make Fun of Ben?

WE USED PLENTY OF CLIPS from CTV's entertainment show *etalk* during our pilot and first week of rehearsal. We discussed at length that we would probably need to use plenty of *etalk* clips in the early stages of production and beyond, because CTV would likely not want to promote *Entertainment Tonight Canada* or other entertainment shows on other networks. It really didn't matter to me because *etalk* host Ben Mulroney was a one-man comedy factory. At one point during a rehearsal show we used a clip of him dressed in drag while he interviewed someone for the Toronto stage version of *Priscilla: Queen of the Desert*. Ben was, quite simply, the ugliest drag queen any of us had ever seen. He was also a very gracious guy who seemed to have no problem with us poking fun at his persona on our show. Something told me Ben had developed a thick skin over the years. The only concern among us was that we might be tempted to use too many clips of Ben from *etalk*.

After our second rehearsal week it was time to prepare for the real thing, and I made my way to the Masonic Temple. It was a Monday and we were supposed to tape our first show that Friday.

The previous week the entire staff had met to go over the rehearsal show and hash out any concerns about content or presentation or, frankly, anything that needed to be corrected before we actually went on the air. We started to discuss content for our first program, and the first thing I asked about were those clips of Ben dressing in drag. They were a week or so out of date, but we weren't concerned with little things like that at this point. We were just trying to make the show as funny as possible, so if the clips weren't 100 percent fresh, so be it. Who cared if the show was called *The Week That Was*?

"So if we're going to use the Ben drag queen clip, should we try to write a better joke for it?" I wondered casually.

"We don't have the rights to use *etalk* clips," said Marla matter-of-factly.

I tried to digest what exactly this person was saying to me.

"What do you mean, *we don't have the rights to use etalk clips*? That show is on CTV, it's a CTV show, don't we have the rights to all CTV shows?"

Marla's answer was a slow, deliberate shake of the head. I was concerned. I was very, very concerned. I asked Michael MacKinnon, our day-to-day show producer, to explain to me why I was just finding out now that we didn't have the rights to use clips from a show that I thought were a mere formality to use. Were other shows like this? Other CTV shows? Turns out the answer was yes.

"So *Marilyn Denis*? We can't use the clips to that show?" I asked.

"Not unless their executive producer gives us the green light," replied Michael.

"So let me get this straight. . ." I was trying to remain calm in front of the entire staff, who likely would not have been surprised had I started throwing things. "You're telling me that in addition to trying to get other networks to let us use their clips, we now have to go to each individual executive producer from each individual in-house production here at CTV and beg them to use their clips as well?"

"Yup, that's pretty much the case," said Michael.

I felt completely duped.

In the previous regime, when Susanne Boyce and Susanne Boyce alone was making programming decisions, the use of such clips would have been a formality. When Susanne or Ivan Fecan green-lit a show, everyone at the network parted the seas to make sure it got on the air the way they wanted.

But I didn't have Susanne in my corner now, and little did I know that Mark and Ben were soon on their way out as well—they no longer had a place in the new Bell world. I had pitched my concept to a regime that was heading out the door, and now I was beginning to realize how truly fucked I was. After the meeting was over I pulled Michael and Brendan aside and asked them to meet with me in an empty office nearby.

"Perhaps," I wondered aloud, "we should consider postponing the show until we have more clips cleared and actual content to write about."

"We can't do that," reasoned Michael. "All of these people will lose their jobs. And besides, we've already started to promote it."

"No one has promoted anything," I replied. "I alone have mentioned it on my Twitter feed. But that's it. That's our promotion. Forget about billboards and radio ads, there aren't even promos for the show running on the actual network the show's appearing on! If you were a regular viewer of MuchMore, you wouldn't even know the show existed. We can easily pull the plug on this."

"But people's jobs . . . " Michael trailed off.

I was so fucked. I was being put in an impossible position. I had pitched a stupid little show that I hoped would develop a cult following over time; now I was being told that about half a dozen people's jobs rested in my hands, and if I backed out now they'd have to find other work. Not to mention the fact that I *really wanted to do the show.* I was at a loss for what to do. My bosses at TSN, Mark Milliere and Ken Volden, were concerned.

"What's going on over there? Are you all right?" Ken asked on the phone one day.

"Not really, I'm kind of fucked. But there's nothing I can do about it because I don't want anyone to be out of work here, and I think eventually we can make a great show. The question is: Will we be given the necessary time to do that, and the resources we need to acquire the content? I'm starting to wonder."

"Keep us posted. We'll pull you off that show if you want."

My lingering Catholic guilt about putting people out of work was too great to pull the chute now. We were going ahead with taping the first show on Friday and airing it on Sunday. The good news was we had a few days to convince *etalk* executive producer Morley Nirenberg to allow us to use clips of Ben. Michael had a great relationship with Morley, and eventually Morley came on board with the idea. I also had a great relationship with *Marilyn Denis Show* executive producer Nan Row, even after I turned down a spot on her show, and I was able to convince her to let us use clips from that show as well.

I took Tuesday off as per usual and planned to be back in the office on Wednesday to go over the script Brendan had written. I was very frustrated that it had taken until four days before the show for me to be told we didn't have access to clips I thought were in the bag, but I needed to maintain a positive front. I wanted everyone on the staff to feel good about the show, and besides, it wasn't as if things could get any worse.

Things were about to get worse. Much, much worse.

CHAPTER 27

We Have Nothing

I ARRIVED AT THE MASONIC TEMPLE offices of *The Week That Was* on Wednesday afternoon with a smile on my face. The weather was sweltering hot, and I loved working downtown instead of making the trek all the way out to Scarborough to work at TSN every night. The Masonic Temple was at Yonge and Davenport, right in the heart of downtown. I envisioned many wonderful years of working there.

But when I walked into our offices that afternoon, it was clear that something was amiss. Michael and Ben were huddled up in an office with Mark McInnis, and they all looked to be discussing something very serious.

I went to say hi to Brendan and everyone else on the staff. We chatted casually about an Internet clip we had planned to use about a Filipino cook named Hot Rod Cantiveros who used to appear on *The Big Breakfast* with me in Winnipeg. Rod had posted a failed pilot on YouTube in which he would "ambush" people at the grocery store, follow them back to their homes with fresh produce, and cook for them and their families. It was just bizarre and unintentionally hilarious and very Canadian. In other words it was exactly the kind of clip we wanted for the show, and lo and behold, Marla had reached Rod's son and gotten approval to actually use the clip! Things were looking up for *The Week That Was*.

It was about that moment when Michael called me into Mark's office. I sat down and saw a look on the faces of those three men that I had never seen before. It was a look of exasperation and defeat. Michael informed me that an executive at another network who had previously agreed to let us use clips from a ton of Canadian reality shows had changed their mind and was now refusing to give us access. These clips made up half of our content and, more importantly, prevented the show from looking like the advertisement for CTV that I had feared it would be.

"We don't have any content!" I screamed, surely getting the attention of the rest of the crew in the offices nearby.

I could not believe this was happening to me. We were scheduled to shoot the first show *in two days* and we had lost *half the show*. It would be like having only the "police" portion of *Law and Order* and not the "district attorney" portion to wrap up the story. We were, to paraphrase a French Revolutionary, *royally fucked*. But I refused to give in.

"What if I went and personally spoke to that executive? I'm really charming in person. This is *not* over yet." I sounded as if I was trying to convince myself.

I was so desperate that I knew I just had to make this work for the sake of the show and for the sake of everyone's jobs. We *needed* those clips. We were too deep in it to quit without a fight. I understood perfectly the position the executive had taken; if I were in charge of that network and someone asked permission to show clips of "funny" moments from their shows, most of which had occurred by accident, I'd have concerns as well. But once we met face-to-face and the executive realized our intention—to celebrate the comic side of Canadian television and not ridicule it—surely, they would agree to let us use those clips. Especially since so many of the clips we had intended to use were brought to my attention by the talent hosting those shows. I was so sure of my ability to convince the executive I was still not yet that discouraged. Ben agreed to accompany me to the executive's office the following day. But first I had to complete my Worldwide Media Tour.

I felt that I had to get the word out somehow, so my friends in the TSN publicity department contacted someone in the MuchMore publicity department. I was paired with a lovely young publicist named Alison Salinas, and we hatched a plan for a quick media blitz with no promotional budget whatsoever. I reached into my own pocket and spent $72 on a monogrammed T-shirt from a store in Kensington Market. I had the guy behind the counter use the old-school 1970s felt letters on a purple T. The front said "JAY ONRAIT WORLDWIDE MEDIA TOUR 2011" and the back said "THE WEEK THAT WAS SUNDAYS ON MUCHMORE." It probably would have been more effective for me to walk around Toronto just wearing that T-shirt like a sandwich board. I intended to wear the shirt during all my interviews. If CTV wasn't going to give me any promos, then I might as well wear one.

Alison booked a few interviews for our worldwide media blitz. The blitz would not in fact be worldwide but consist only of CTV-owned and -produced shows: *CP24 Breakfast, Canada AM*, and *etalk*. Yes, the irony was not lost on me that I was about to promote my show on other TV shows whose clips I wasn't originally allowed to use on my own show. We would also make a quick stop on *Off the Record with Michael Landsberg* on TSN before I went across town to try to beg the TV executive to not kill half our show content. This was all going to happen within the space of a few hours.

Meanwhile, back at *The Week That Was* offices, Brendan was

busy trying to write sketches, and the other show producers were searching frantically for usable clips that could fill time if we weren't successful in convincing the executive to change their mind about the clips. We were scheduled to shoot at noon the next day.

I should have walked away right then and there. Before I even went on the Worldwide Media Tour I should have politely explained to the entire staff why this concept could no longer work. The show I had conceived and pitched was not the show we would be putting on MuchMore that Sunday. But a combination of (a) my stupidity and (b) my blind confidence that I could convince anyone to give me what I wanted kept me going that day and kept me encouraged as I prepared for the meeting.

My interviews on *CP24 Breakfast*, *Canada AM*, and *etalk* went extremely well. The hosts could not have been more kind about the project and seemed genuinely enthusiastic. I performed some bizarre pratfall on *CP24 Breakfast* and pretended to hit on *etalk* correspondent Danielle McGimsie for laughs. *Off the Record* was an even better experience. Michael Landsberg is, in many ways, my hero.

I had met Michael years before during my very first year at Ryerson, two years before I started at the network. I was given an assignment to contact someone in the Canadian broadcast industry whom I admired and wanted to interview. Michael came to mind right away because he was hosting the show I wanted to host some-day: *Sportsdesk*. I called the TSN offices, then located on Sheppard Avenue in North York, and was amazingly put through to Michael's voice mail. Keep in mind this was pre-Internet, so a cold call was the only way to go into this situation, just like *What Color Is Your Parachute?* had taught me all those years before.

Unbelievably, Michael called me in my dorm room at Pitman Hall in Ryerson the following day. He was *very* Michael Landsberg, which I mean in the best way possible. I probably get asked about

Michael more than any other TSN personality, and the questions about him are usually posted in a negative way: "Is he a jerk in real life?" "Is he as arrogant as he seems?" The answer is always no. In fact, Michael has always been one of the most kind, generous, and supportive people at TSN. On the phone that day back at Ryerson, he invited me to shadow him at TSN for an evening while he worked, and he said we could complete the interview while he was preparing for the show. I couldn't believe it. The experience was truly amazing. Michael had also attended Ryerson, and we talked about how he managed to land at TSN. He let me watch the show live from the studio and offered to help if I ever wanted to apply for work there someday. I never forgot how kind he was.

That afternoon when I went to be interviewed by Michael for my fledgling little TV project, I was once again reminded that not everyone working in the Canadian TV industry was trying to keep me from reaching my goals. Before we sat down for the interview, I explained all the issues I had been having trying to clear clips for the show and the roadblocks in front of me. He immediately gave me permission to use any clip from *Off the Record* that I wanted. He flat-out encouraged me to make fun of him and his show for the sake of my own show, though he pointed out that he would be sure to give it back just as good. I honestly wanted to hug him. I thought I might break down and cry. For a moment, I thought everything was going to be all right.

Then I walked into the meeting with the executive.

I knew the entire fate and future of our show was probably riding on this meeting. I had yet to meet the executive with whom we would be meeting that day. As you've probably guessed, I'm withholding the name of that executive and will continue to do so as I describe this meeting that fateful afternoon. There are several reasons for this, but the main one is that I am not ready to take on another profession. As Mike Bullard learned the hard way, this is a small industry. I'm not interested in burning bridges. I don't want to get overly dramatic, but for the purposes of this account I will refer to this executive as "the Dreamcrusher."

I met my executive producer, Ben, in the lobby of the Dreamcrusher's building, and we went over our plan. Ben was not confident that we could get access to all the clips we had intended to use, so our strategy was to try to get the least offensive ones. I also mentioned that I would offer to personally travel up to the Dreamcrusher's offices at least once a week to go over clips that we intended to use, even offering scripts and jokes for approval. It was a deal I didn't think any reasonable human being could turn down.

But I wasn't dealing with a reasonable human being. I was dealing with the Dreamcrusher, and I knew we were in trouble as soon as we walked into the office.

CHAPTER 28

The Dreamcrusher

THE DREAMCRUSHER WAS ON the phone, back turned to us, and remained that way for about a minute while Ben and I made funny faces at each other. Usually a person hosting a meeting in this situation might turn around, acknowledge the people in the office, and raise one finger to say, "Just a second, gentlemen, I'll be right with you." I began to wonder if maybe the Dreamcrusher had forgotten about us, even though they had summoned us to the office. *Was this some sort of intimidation tactic?* I wondered. *I really should be helping to write jokes right now.*

Suddenly, the Dreamcrusher spun around and faced us.

"Where are my flowers, guys?"

"Uh..." I stumbled before quickly realizing what the Dreamcrusher was referring to.

I had brought a bouquet of flowers with me to the set of *Canada AM* that morning for my interview with Bev Thomson as a peace offering for all the funny clips I had hoped to use of her, though really it was just a simple little sight gag. The Dreamcrusher had seen the interview. "I can run out and grab some flowers right now!" I offered cheerfully. But the Dreamcrusher was no longer interested in talking flowers and quickly moved on to the next subject. The Dreamcrusher was about to crush dreams.

"Guys, here's the deal . . . " began the Dreamcrusher.

I leaned forward in anticipation.

"You will get nothing."

"I'm sorry?" I replied.

"You will get nothing. No clips from any of our shows. Nothing. All of those clips are off limits."

"Okay, hold on . . . " Ben started, but the Dreamcrusher was not finished.

"Sorry, guys, I'm not budging on this. I can't have the reputations of my talent compromised in any way."

It took every ounce of my strength to remain calm. "You do realize that your talent sent us many of the clips we intended to use? We have some great stuff that we think will make your talent even more popular." Even as the words came out of my mouth, I knew the Dreamcrusher wasn't buying the argument.

"Forget it," replied the Dreamcrusher. "You guys want to make fun of us, and it's not going to happen. I don't care who sent you the clips. What happens if you play one of our clips featuring one of our hosts and it goes viral?"

"They . . . become even more popular?" I replied.

Surely, several funny clips from the Dreamcrusher's shows had already appeared on YouTube by this point. There was no stopping funny clips from going viral. Did this person realize that a funny clip from a show "going viral" was a good thing? Apparently not. This person was a television person and was above the concept of clips "going viral." This person had absolutely no intention of being a team player. I wanted to throw something at this person so badly.

"No, I'm not going to let you guys embarrass us," the Dream-crusher replied.

"What if," I reasoned, "I drove up here to your offices once, twice a week and we went over the clips we intend to use together, and you can voice your concerns or ask us to make any changes you like? I'll even bring you scripts and jokes so you can make sure nothing will embarrass any of your talent. We can even talk to the talent!"

"I don't have time for that," the Dreamcrusher stated matter-of-factly. The Dreamcrusher was ready to wrap this meeting up. I looked over at Ben. He continued to try to reason with the Dreamcrusher, but it was clear the Dreamcrusher had never intended to be reasoned with. The trip had been a complete waste of time. Ben and I stood up and walked out without saying good-bye; it was as polite as I could have possibly been in the situation.

As I drove back downtown to my condo after saying a dejected goodbye to Ben, I started to have revenge fantasies.

The first thing I fantasized about was taking a shit on the Dreamcrusher's car while it sat in the parking lot of the studio build-ing. *How would I get away with it without people seeing me?* I won-dered. Could I possibly shit in a bag and then dump the shit on the Dreamcrusher's car? Maybe I could just wipe my own shit on the nameplate that hung over the Dreamcrusher's parking stall. I'm not sure why I was so obsessed with defacing the Dreamcrusher's prop-erty with shit—I was never very imaginative when it came to pranks.

I also considered actually spray-painting the outside of the Dreamcrusher's office with some sort of creative tag like "asshole," but then I realized all I'd be doing in that situation was making a bunch of work for the custodial staff at the network. I soon came to the conclusion that I was being childish and I needed to "park it." I was so frustrated with the Dreamcrusher for refusing to even be reasonable in this situation that I was thinking irrationally. Luckily, my thoughts did not turn into actions, and thankfully I haven't seen the Dreamcrusher since. I highly doubt the Dreamcrusher gave the meeting a second thought.

We were flat-out screwed. Losing half our content one day before taping the show forced us to use clips from shows that had aired, in some cases, several months ago. Many of those clips were from American shows that had surprisingly given us access. The clips were okay, and the fact that their producers had given us access was truly appreciated, but the truth is I was gutted. I had not intended to use clips from American shows at all; what would have been the point of that? I was trying to do everything I possibly could to separate ourselves from *The Soup*; instead, we were looking more and more like *The Soup* every day. The show was supposed to be a celebration of all things *Canadian*; instead, I was being undone by Canadians who were too sensitive to be made fun of. In other words, I was being undone by the one thing that makes Canadians so Canadian. Damn Canadians!

We had intended to try to write some sketches involving people around the office: "show behind the show" sketches pioneered by my hero on *Late Night with David Letterman*. We thought we might try to introduce such sketches after the two-week break for the Kraft Celebration Tour as a new and funny element that would take the show to the next level. Instead, because of the dearth of actual clips we now had to work with, we needed actual content that we could shoot and edit in less than twenty-four hours.

There just happened to be a massive heat wave that week in Toronto, and Bell Media had sent out a company memo to all employees encouraging everyone to go ahead and wear "summer-appropriate attire" because of the rising temperatures. Quickly seizing the opportunity in front of us, we wrote a sketch that would fill time and hopefully shock people a little bit. The premise of the sketch was that after reading the company-wide memo, I arrived at work in what I considered to be "summer-appropriate attire": completely naked except for one of those floppy women's summer hats you'd imagine ladies wearing in a stage production of *The Great Gatsby*.

To achieve this effect, I walked a few blocks down Yonge Street to the massive three-storey sex shop, Seduction, known in Toronto as the Walmart of sex shops. There I bought a flesh-coloured thong (Caucasian flesh of course), though they only had one in a medium. My penis and balls were squished into that thing like a jack-in-the-box, and it was not flattering. I don't consider myself well-endowed by any stretch, but the combination of full-blast air conditioning combined with the tiny thong made my penis and testicles look like bait in a tackle box. There were several women on staff, and they all must have been thinking the same thing: "So, it's true: Tall, skinny guys have small wieners."

I didn't care. In fact, it was fairly liberating to put my modest junk on display in the name of a few much-needed laughs both behind the scenes and on-camera. I wasn't completely thrilled with the way the sketch turned out, not because of my compacted genitalia, but because we simply didn't have the time to write or edit something that would have been more worthy of a first show. We were left with no choice.

The next day we taped our first episode. Spirits were high, and the entire crew joined us as our "audience," much the same way *The Soup* used their crew as a makeshift audience to provide laughter. We had all been through a pretty damn rough week, and I think everyone just wanted to be done with episode 1 and hope things got better for episode 2. I tried to abide by my mom's favourite piece of advice: "Do the best you can with what you have."

Viewership was low, like 8,000 people for the first viewing, 24,000 for the second. To put this in perspective: If an hour of *SportsCentre* got 8,000 viewers, my bosses at TSN would probably commit suicide. Expectations were lower at a station like

MuchMore, which didn't have the viewership of TSN, but the writing was on the wall. We weren't getting promoted, and therefore we weren't getting viewers, and we weren't even doing the show we wanted to do in the first place. We were screwed.

After the first show aired most of the feedback we received was negative, but much of it surprisingly did not centre on the content of the show; instead people were annoyed by the small studio audience. It just confused the hell out of them. We kept getting requests to either make the audience bigger or forget the audience altogether. I had underestimated how few people in Canada had actually seen *The Soup*.

We decided to play off those complaints, and I used my relationship with the very kind executive producer of *Marilyn*, Nan Row, to set up a sketch with me "stealing" some of the audience waiting to walk into the studio to see a taping of *Marilyn* and taking them over to my show. It worked really well, and I was so grateful to Nan and Marilyn for trying to help us out.

Another time-filler sketch involved me auditioning to be the in-game arena host for the Toronto Maple Leafs. Then Maple Leafs GM Brian Burke even sent me an e-mail wishing me luck on the sketch and apologizing for not being around to make a cameo. What a guy! My spirits were lifted somewhat, but we were getting no closer to having more clips to use on the show. Comedian Brent Butt from *Corner Gas* graciously agreed to record a fake voice mail for the show to use in another sketch, working for free while he was busy on other projects. Other than the sketches, our shows consisted of the same clips over and over from the same shows that would allow us to lampoon them: *etalk, Marilyn, 1 Girl 5 Gays*. In other words, only CTV shows. My vow to not let *The Week That Was* turn into a half-hour commercial for CTV was failing miserably. I was also exhausted. The whole point of doing a clip show was to allow me to have the time to work at *SportsCentre* and not be wasted at the end of the week. Now I was getting up early and working on sketches after hosting on TSN the night before. I knew I couldn't keep up this pace unless we were able to secure some more clips, but all we kept hearing was "We'll pass it on to our lawyers and see what they say."

I had really, really blown it. I should have spent about a year clearing clips behind the scenes with other broadcasters. Now we were stuck doing what was essentially a sketch show without a sketch troupe and just one writer. Something had to give. There would be times when Brendan and I would come up with a concept based on a clip from a Canadian show. We'd get halfway through writing it, and then we'd remember to look over to Marla to see if we had permission to use the clip. She would never answer verbally, just slowly shake her head from side to side to indicate there was no chance to clear the clip in time for our show taping that Friday. I came to despise that head shake almost as much as I despised the Dreamcrusher. The problem was that I didn't have to deal with the Dreamcrusher anymore, but the head shake I had to deal with several times a day, every day. Roadblocks were all we saw in front of us. We weren't trying to take anyone down, we weren't trying to ruin anyone's career, we just wanted to make a funny little Canadian show, and it just wasn't happening.

We finished our four shows for the summer, barely, and then I prepared to head west for year three of the Kraft Celebration Tour. I normally looked forward to the Kraft Tour anyway, but this was an especially needed break. Dan and I and the rest of the crew hopped on a flight to Kelowna, about a two-hour drive from Armstrong, B.C., where the tour was scheduled to begin. As the plane landed, I did what every single person does on a plane that lands anywhere in the world these days: I powered up my phone and went to check my messages. The first thing I noticed in my inbox was a company-wide memo sent from the head of

CTV Specialty programming. I clicked on the e-mail and scrolled through it. Then my jaw hit the floor.

The gist of the memo was that Mark McInnis and Ben Rotterman were being let go from the company after many long years of service. Yes, the same Mark and Ben who had approved the original pitch and overseen the entire thing. The same Mark and Ben who were in charge of my show. There was no mention of my show in the memo, but the bottom line was pretty clear: It was over for *The Week That Was.*

I felt, to be perfectly honest, a sense of relief. I could not have kept the show going in its current format. It wasn't funny enough, and it wasn't close enough to the show I really wanted to do. I thought we might be given a year to find our way like all network shows need these days (see: *Late Night with Jimmy Fallon*), but I knew we weren't going to get the resources we needed anyway.

I thought I knew the mechanism of CTV shows. I also thought that if I kept the operation small, practically a secret, I might be able to hang on to creative control and create something I was really proud of. But it backfired; instead, we were like a forgotten entity, and the people in charge were halfway out the door by the time we hit production. I should have been more diligent in making sure we had access to the content we needed, because that was the entire purpose of the show. Had I realized the show would turn into half a sketch show, I might have pushed to hire more sketch comedians. But I didn't want to do a sketch show, I wanted to do a clip show, and not having access to those clips was just the beginning of our many issues.

Even in moments when I chastise myself for not being in *The Week That Was* production offices full time, I realize that realistically I could not have approached the show any other way. I haven't talked about how much money I was making to do the show, but let's just say that baristas in Toronto are probably pulling in more in

Jay Onrait

tips. There was no way I could simply quit *SportsCentre* and go full time on *The Week That Was* unless I wanted to drastically change my lifestyle, which at this point in my life I didn't want to do. I know it's not very "artist" of me but it's the truth. I liked my lifestyle, I loved hosting *SportsCentre*, and I wasn't willing to give that up to take a chance on a show on MuchMore. In the end, that was obviously the one correct choice I made.

In all, it was a great lesson for me when it comes to putting together a TV show: I needed to be better prepared, to make sure all the bases were covered—it was *my* name on the show after all. I was just so happy that I was finally doing *something* with my spare time following the Olympics that I skimmed over the details. Luckily, not much damage was done to my career, and to this day people still tell me they actually liked the show and wished it was still on. I wish it was still on, too, in the format that I had intended. Every year new shows like *Canada's Got Talent*, *The Bachelor Canada*, and *Amazing Race Canada* launch to great publicity across this great nation, and they are just waiting to be skewered. It makes me wonder what might have been.

I see members of our crew for lunch on occasion, and they're all doing very well. I suppose I shouldn't have stressed so much about keeping their jobs alive, because they were all so talented there was no question they'd land on their feet. We kick back and reminisce about that one crazy summer in 2011 when we all tried to put a show on Canadian TV and came up just short. Better to have tried and failed than not to have tried at all, I guess. Maybe someday some or all of us will be able to work together again. I'm pondering new ideas.

CHAPTER 29

The Last Sportscaster of the Year

UNDER NO CIRCUMSTANCES DID I ever think I would win an award for my achievements in broadcasting. I knew that several of our most talented hosts, writers, and producers had won Geminis in the past, including my friend and *NHL on TSN* host James Duthie, who had been nominated for several Geminis before finally getting a well-deserved win in 2009. I used to chide him on-air about being a multiple Gemini nominee who was always the bridesmaid but never the bride. Truthfully, it always kind of irked me that CBC personalities seemed to traditionally dominate the event. It obviously irked CTV News so much that they pulled themselves out of Gemini consideration altogether. I had always assumed my broadcasting style was considered too weird and out there for Gemini voters, so imagine my surprise when I was nominated for Best Sportscaster of the Year in 2010, the summer after my Vancouver Olympics stint.

The exposure from the Olympics had obviously helped my cause and brought me to the attention of Gemini voters, and I was grateful for the nomination if for no other reason than I might be able to use it as a bargaining chip in future contract negotiations. I was up against two people who worked for my own company: the aforementioned Mr. Duthie and CTV Olympic host Brian Williams (I am contractually obligated to introduce him that way), so it was obvious from the very beginning that I would never, ever win the actual award if those two were nominated in my category. Also nominated was a local CBC Vancouver sportscaster named Shane Foxman. In the end we all lost out to Mr. Duthie, who was surprised that he had won over Mr. Williams although he shouldn't have been. I was happy that James was finally getting the recognition he deserved from others in the industry. Had I actually won the award that year, I'm pretty sure the entire method of awarding Geminis would have been stripped down and re-evaluated. As it turns out, that wouldn't happen until I actually did win the award a year later.

The year after the Olympics was a relatively quiet one in the industry and especially at TSN. I had been concentrating on trying to get *The Week That Was* off the ground and had not pursued any new sports ventures other than continuing to host *SportsCentre* with Dan every night. However, I had been really proud of the direction Dan and I were taking with the show and truly grateful to my bosses for giving us free rein to make *SportsCentre* into more of a hybrid comedy/sports program. That summer, Comedy Central in the United States launched two separate attempts at doing a show for sports along the lines of *The Daily Show*. One was *Onion SportsDome*, which was produced by the creators of the satirical online news site The Onion. That show was attempting to take the piss out of sports highlight shows in general, and I thought it had some pretty funny moments, but ultimately it did not last.

Also launching in the summer of 2011 was *Sports Show with Norm MacDonald*, starring the Canadian comedian and former *SNL* "Weekend Update" host. To this day I am amazed it is not still on the air. It was clearly cheap to produce, and I thought it was reasonably funny and would have only gotten better as MacDonald found his groove. My only complaint was that the show was almost a little *too much* Norm, and this is coming from a *huge* Norm MacDonald fan. Probably because of budgetary constraints, Norm not only did a "Weekend Update"–style set of headlines to kick off the show but also went into the field and did stories as well. I thought a little less Norm would have gone a long way: He could have hosted the headlines segment and then passed it on to a couple of reporters who could do the field pieces, sort of the same format as *The Daily Show*. Alas, just like *The Week That Was*, *Sports Show* was never given the chance to find its footing, and it was cancelled after just ten episodes.

Dan and I were continuing to push the envelope on *SportsCentre*, starting to ad lib around highlights more and write introductory on-cams that were closer to comedy sketches than sports journalism. A little novice hockey player who was taking too long to make a lap around the ice holding a Red Wings flag before a regular-season game was told, "GET OFF THE ICE, YOU LITTLE BRAT!" I made allusions to never quitting my job, telling the viewers they would have to "drag my dead corpse out of here." I screamed at the viewers at full volume that we were showing NHL pre-season hockey and they should "WATCH IT! WATCH IT!" I basically spent the entirety of 2011 screaming at our viewers on live television, and many of them seemed to enjoy it.

Meanwhile, we were continuing to host the *SportsCentre Morning Rush* on TSN2 throughout the summer, a show I began every day by screaming, "*Ohhhhhhhhhhhhh . . . . whatta RUSSSSSSSSSSSSSSSSSSHHHH!!!*" as an homage to the entrance music that the Road Warriors tag team used back in the day in the WWF and the NWA. Occasionally, our bosses would tell us to "dial it back 10 percent," but for the most part we were given carte blanche to continue cultivating these crazy antics, and I was getting closer to turning our show into what I always wanted it to be: a true late-night talk show/sports highlight show hybrid, but without those annoying guests. All killer, no filler!

I had made the assumption that, because there were no Olympics to speak of and I had hosted no other major events in 2011, my Gemini nomination was a one-and-done situation. I wasn't even thinking about it, really. So imagine my surprise when I was told I had indeed been nominated for Sportscaster of the Year once again, alongside Mr. Foxman, and my colleague Darren Dutchyshen.

This created a somewhat awkward situation: Dutchy is a personal hero of mine and probably the biggest single reason I wanted to get into broadcasting when I was a kid. The idea of being nominated for an award beside him was a truly humbling and rewarding experience, but the idea of actually *winning* the award at his expense made me completely uncomfortable. Dutchy alleviated the situation by saying he hoped one of us would win it so that the award would stay in the family. I truly appreciated that.

The evening of the award show, TSN had booked three tables full of writers, producers, talent, and executives, and I took my place among them. Dutchy was sitting at my table, and I ran into Shane Foxman before the ceremony began. He was a truly kind and gracious guy and a real talent with a unique style. I suppose I thought of him as a bit of a kindred spirit. I really didn't want an awkward situation, not to mention the fact that as someone who had admired Dutchy all his life, I truly believed he deserved to be rewarded for all his years of hard work. In the end, I pretended not to care as they announced that I'd won. Dutchy came over and gave me a big hug and told me he was proud of me.

I meandered up on stage to give my thank you speech, being careful to thank my bosses and giving my own tribute to the network: I spun around at one point and revealed that the letters *TSN* had been shaved into the back of my head, pointing out that

I would never be able to leave the company after such a stunt. (I had just returned from the Kraft Tour, and during the last stop in MacGregor, Manitoba, a young hairdresser was shaving *TSN* into little kids' heads for fun, so I asked her to do it for me as well.)

I also made sure I saved the most important two people for last in my speech: Producer Tim, whom I acknowledged for "keeping us from getting fired every single night," and Dan, whom I credited in all sincerity with being a better broadcaster than I was. I tried to pretend it didn't matter, but just like any award it doesn't suck when you're acknowledged for what you do. My bosses were happy, I was happy, and I started to tuck into a double vodka and prepare for what would be a celebratory night. Good thing I never had to work early. The next morning was probably going to be pretty painful.

Then I checked my phone.

A text from Dan: "Where are you?"

"Um, at the Geminis?" I texted back. "I won! Just getting the skill saw out and preparing to cut it in half for you."

"Oh, that's great," replied Dan. "You do realize you're working tonight, right?"

"What?" I asked.

"Your name is on the schedule. Everyone is wondering where you are. You're scheduled to work."

I pondered this for a moment, silently, while my Gemini award was passed around among my peers. Surely TSN would not have scheduled me to work on the same night as the Gemini Awards, would they?

Turns out they would.

And they did.

I wandered over to *SportsCentre* executive producer Steve Argintaru, who was not in charge of scheduling the hosts for the show and at least pretended to be as surprised as I was. One of my two immediate bosses, vice-president of news and information Ken

Volden, was also surprised, but neither of them were exactly floating the idea of me taking the night off. I had to shake off my buzz, sober up with a few big pieces of stale dinner roll, and get my ass in to work. I probably shouldn't have driven myself in, but my mind was racing and I didn't want to be the guy who made my producer call another anchor in to work on the show at the last minute because I was getting drunk.

On the way to work I formulated an idea for the opening of the show that night. Word had already travelled back to the newsroom about my win that evening. As soon as I arrived, after receiving many wonderful congratulations from everyone in our newsroom, I sought out our biggest and burliest writer: Guy Desormeaux, who looked like a guy who would have done a mean clean and jerk at the 1952 Olympics.

"Could you carry me?" I asked Guy. "Like, in your arms?"

He laughed at me. Yes, he could carry my scrawny ass, probably for miles without much effort.

That night the show opened with Dan sitting alone at the desk, commenting on the fact that he would likely be hosting the show alone that evening and that he had no idea where I was. Suddenly, triumphant orchestral music played and I emerged—carried onto the set in the arms of Guy, who let me down gently in my seat.

"Could you get me a cucumber water?" I called out to Guy as he left the set.

"Nice to know this win hasn't gone to your head," said Dan.

Dan suggested later that I keep the Gemini in my fridge as opposed to on a coffee table or a mantle. His reasoning was that if I had people over and they went to the fridge to grab a beer they would be met with a pleasant surprise. About two weeks later the *Toronto Star* contacted our communications department and asked if any of our recent Gemini winners kept their trophies in an unusual place. Our communications manager, Chobi Liang, whom

I had recently started dating, informed them that I kept my Gemini in the fridge. Next thing I knew, the paper had sent over one of their staff photographers to take a picture. He set up the camera in the back of the fridge and got a great shot of me reaching for a beer with the Gemini in the foreground. The beer company saw it, and I got free beer out of that shot. It may have been a greater accomplishment than the Gemini win.

A year later I was told that the Gemini committee was consolidating several awards and that Best Sportscaster was being eliminated. I tried to pretend it wasn't because the Gemini committee had concluded they'd made a major mistake in giving me the award the previous year, but it probably was. And I am very much okay with that. Either way, they can't take away the statue in my fridge. The beer, however, is long gone.

CHAPTER 30

Pooping in an Old Man's Apartment

THE KRAFT CELEBRATION TOUR was supposed to be a one-time thing, a chance to celebrate the network's twenty-fifth anniversary in the summer of 2009 by travelling across the country and putting on our show in front of a live audience. TSN viewers were encouraged to nominate their community, and those nominations were eventually whittled down to two per province. Then, those two nominated communities went head-to-head in a direct voting competition, with the community that collected the most votes declared the winner until we ended up with ten stops across the country. One crew, led by Darren Dutchyshen and Jennifer Hedger, would travel westward; the other crew, led by Dan and me, would go east. We would put on five shows each. The first year was such a success that despite the fact it was supposed to be a one-time thing to celebrate our network's anniversary, TSN and Kraft decided to extend it for two more years, and then another three years after that.

Dan and I looked forward to the start of the Kraft Tour like kids waiting for Christmas morning. The first year, a crew of about twenty crammed into one bus; by year three, the crew had expanded to about forty and we had three buses. The country's very best sports production freelancers all vie to get on the tour, not just because of the money but also because it's a hell of a lot of fun to be on a road trip like this one. Although it's always a damn good party, we also put on an outstanding show in every town. The smaller the community, the more fun the shows tend to be. Everyone in town rallies around the event, and we try to make it as memorable as possible.

We usually ask the organizing committee to suggest some activities that Dan and I can participate in that might be unique to the town or area. In the past, such activities have included hanging off a speedboat as it powers down the North Saskatchewan River near Devon, Alberta; racing combines at the Agricultural Museum near MacGregor, Manitoba (I lost); and shooting watermelons from a cannon and milking goats against the clock near Armstrong, B.C. (I lost again and had to drink the milk in my pail—pretty good actually).

The activities are always a lot of fun but never as much fun as the show itself: a real outdoor rock stage, usually set up in the middle of the community, with giant screens projecting the show for all to see. Our backs were facing the audience so we could have the crowd in the background on TV, but early on Dan and I decided we needed to turn around and acknowledge the crowd as much as possible before the show and during commercial breaks. We wanted to make it a real show, not just another edition of *SportsCentre*, so about an hour before we go live across the country, Dan and I hopped on stage and started dancing, singing, and generally trying to get the crowd to go as crazy as possible. We loved to get everyone to sing along with us to "Don't Stop Believin'" by Journey and "Livin' on a Prayer" by Bon Jovi, as well as whatever new songs were hitting the charts that year. Every stop we made was so much fun, and it was a truly unique way to see this massive country we lived in. Not to mention the lifelong friendships we made with our outstanding crew members along the way. It was one of my favourite parts of the job.

Our third stop on the 2012 Kraft Tour was Bathurst, New Brunswick. It ended up being one of our best-ever crowds, around 3,000 people lining the water just off the downtown strip. We were treated like royalty from the second we arrived. They whisked us around town and took us to the Big D diner for lunch. A classic old-school burger joint that first opened in 1969, it was the kind of place where waitresses in roller skates would bring food out to your car as you waited. They are still bringing food to your cars at Big D, but the roller skates are long gone. We also stopped at McLean's Fish Shop and were promptly shown the proper way to crack open and eat a lobster, the owner promising to ship me lobsters in less than twenty-four hours if I called him directly. The stop was shaping up to be one of our best.

The day of the event, Dan and I woke early and went to a local radio station for a quick interview followed by an autograph signing at a local Superstore that was so poorly attended the store manager apologized to us. I just told him it was good preparation for my eventual book tour, when I would be sitting with stacks of *Anchorboy* and looking forlorn as customers lined up with their copies of *Fifty Shades of Grey* and ignored me.

We had stopped at the Big D diner for the second time in two days, and by the time I arrived at the show site I, uh, really had to go *number two*. (Sorry, trying to make this as pleasant as possible to read. I realize you've already had to sit through a chapter about poop in this book.)

Dan is always adamant that he will never do a "road trip"— that is, have a bowel movement anywhere other than home or in his own hotel room. I just do not have the physiological makeup to put things off that way. So, I was faced with a bit of a conundrum. There were porta-potties, but I don't think I need to explain why that idea was disgusting. There were toilets on the tour buses, but using them for anything other than *number one* was a complete and absolute non-starter—the worst violation anyone on the tour could commit. On the first year of the tour, someone dared break that rule and went *number two* on the bus, back when we had only one bus and not three. To this day, no one on the crew has fessed up to the crime, but Dan witnessed the rage that the bus driver displayed upon learning that someone had dared soil his septic system with solid waste. The culprit would probably have been better off to just shit on the bus driver's face.

That afternoon, however, nature called and she was not about to be ignored. Near the show site I noticed a cluster of industrial-looking buildings, and outside of one of them three gentlemen were gathered at a picnic table enjoying their lunch al fresco. Surely they wouldn't mind my using their company washroom, especially if they were all outside for the next hour. I gingerly approached them and hoped I wouldn't be recognized. I could just imagine the stories now: "Onrait was in Bathurst last week. He took a dump in our bathroom. It was epic!"

As I said, I hoped I would not be recognized. I approached the picnic table.

"Onrait!" yelled the oldest of the three men.

So much for that.

I thought "Guys, can I please drop the kids off in your pool?" was perhaps a little uncouth, so instead I broached the subject with a bit more trepidation.

"Hey, guys, coming over to watch the show today?"

"You bet! Do you think you could get me a T-shirt? I opened the gate for the buses and trucks when they first arrived," said the oldest gentleman again. The other two guys at the table were around my age, but the self-designated orator of the group looked slightly older than my parents, somewhere close to seventy perhaps.

"I wish I could, my friend, but *I* can't even get one of those T-shirts." This probably sounded like an outright lie, but it was actually true. Those T-shirts were harder to come by than a Honus Wagner rookie card. "I *could* get you a hat, however, but I need to ask you a favour. Do you think I could use the company washroom? Ours is a bit crowded right now." I tried to force a laugh at that point.

"Sure!" replied the older man immediately.

Wow, that was easy! What a nice guy. I glanced over at the picnic table and noticed there were six empty beer cans, and they were each working on their third brew of the break. *Wish we had these relaxed rules about drinking during our lunch break!* I thought to myself.

"I can show you where it is," said the older gentleman.

"That's so not necessary. Just point me in the right direction and I will be out of your hair in a minute," I offered. But the old man was having none of it. He wanted to talk about TSN and the show and whether I really couldn't get him one of those Kraft T-shirts, and I was happy to oblige in some idle chatter for the chance to use a real washroom. He was clearly a hard-working, hard-living guy, and I wanted him to remember me as someone who took the time to chat for a minute or so before soiling his company's likely pristine washroom facilities. We entered the building and he led me upstairs to what I assumed were his offices. I had neglected to ask what he and the other two fellas actually *did* for a living, but I made the assumption that since we were in an industrial park, it had to do with auto parts or construction or something else I would never understand. The old man walked a few steps ahead of me.

"My place is just up here."

Your place?

"I live alone, so it's a bit messy in my apartment."

Your apartment?

Was I really about to take a shit in an old man's apartment?

It appeared that, yes, I was about to take a shit in an old man's apartment.

But there were other questions: Was I walking toward my impending death? Was I about to be chopped up into little pieces and thrown into the harbour? How would anyone from TSN ever find me here? Perhaps more importantly, how would Dan do the show all by himself?

I figured now was a good time to abort the mission. I called out to him as he made his way up the final steps to the third floor, his floor. "I'm so sorry, I didn't realize this was your apartment building. I thought you worked here. I sincerely apologize. I should probably get going." At this point those porta-potties were looking pretty good.

"Nah! Don't sweat it. You might as well use it. I'm not using it!" he said with a laugh. This logic made a surprising amount of sense to me at the time. I followed him toward his front door. This was really happening. "Stranger Shit 2012" was on.

What was the worst that could happen? That he might kill me and leave me for dead? I realized it was actually pretty difficult to tell from the appearance of a person whether this was a possibility unless that person was wearing a hockey mask and you were at a summer camp. I decided to just go for it, finish the job as quickly as possible, run back to the show site, get him a hat, and pretend this entire thing had never happened.

He opened the door to his apartment.

Now the porta-potties were starting to look like bathrooms at the Bellagio.

The place was, for lack of a better term, an absolute pigsty. It had likely never been cleaned in the entire time he had lived there. Open cans of food and empty cans of beer littered the filthy kitchen. The stale smell of smoke, lager, and musty newspapers and magazines permeated the air and hit my olfactory nerves like a rocket. It smelled exactly like my grandfather's basement, only this place didn't fill me with memories of my childhood. This was likely the place I was going to die.

At least the smell of my rotting corpse wouldn't affect the neighbours too much. It would probably be weeks before they noticed. By then the Kraft Tour would be over, and Dan and my other fellow employees would have assumed I had simply abandoned the company to marry a Maritime girl and lead a simpler life in New Brunswick as a morning radio DJ.

The old man led me through the small, extremely cluttered one bedroom. Hockey cards were everywhere, and literally hundreds of hats. Baseball hats to be specific.

"I collect them," he said. "I have a few worth a lot of money."

Perhaps the old man's love of collecting baseball caps would be the one thing that kept me alive that afternoon. I made sure he knew what was waiting for him if I lived through this ordeal. "I've got a TSN hat with your name on it! I just have to go back to the show site and pick it up." I was trying to dangle a carrot in front of him in the hopes he wouldn't kill me. I just wanted to poop and leave. I was actually going to do this. I was going to have a bowel movement in a complete stranger's dirty bathroom.

And it *was* dirty.

"Take your time; I'll be out here," he said.

"Sounds good, thanks!" I replied. This was turning into some bizarre *SNL* sketch. As soon as I shut the door to the loo, I realized he was not going to make his way to the other side of the apartment. Instead, he decided to continue our conversation as I sat on his throne.

"So, have you ever met Wayne Gretzky?" Yes, I had met Wayne Gretzky, I replied, as I glanced over at where the roll of toilet paper *should* have been.

The holder was completely empty. There was one dirty towel flung over the shower. This was a dire situation. "Ever interviewed Sidney Crosby? We love Sid in the Maritimes," he continued.

Was this really my life? I continued the conversation as if there wasn't a door separating us while I pooped in his toilet and wondered how I was going to wipe myself. By now the rest of the crew were probably also wondering where I had disappeared to. Why didn't I just crap my pants? At that point I really, really wished I had crapped my pants.

As I finished my business, I realized there was only one option.

I flushed the toilet—thank God *that* was working—and I hopped up on his bathroom counter, sat directly in his sink, and turned on the water. Then, employing a method used by millions of people in South Asia and other parts of the world, I used the hands-and-water technique to clean my undercarriage.

"Everything okay in there?" the old man called out.

"Just great, thanks," I replied.

Yeah, just great. This is *exactly* what I had envisioned when I entered the Canadian television business: sitting in the filthy sink of a filthy bathroom cleaning my filthy ass while having a conversation with a complete stranger and potential serial killer on the other side of the door. This must be what people were referring to when they talked about "the Golden Age of Television."

I finished cleaning up and was grateful to see a bar of soap on the counter. After washing up, I realized there was nothing I could use to dry my hands or my undercarriage. I pulled up my shorts anyway and immediately decided this was better than having *not* cleaned myself at all. Then I exited the bathroom to find the old man staring straight at me. "Everything okay?" he asked.

"Everything is great, thanks so much!" I replied. A more honest conversation would have gone something like this:

"Did you just take a dump in my toilet and then clean your ass in my sink?"

"Why, yes, I sure did; thanks for the opportunity to do that!"

The old man was insistent that he have the chance to show

me some of his most "valuable" baseball caps, including a vintage Labatt Lite cap. I patiently listened while he informed me about the ups and downs of the vintage baseball cap industry in our country, all the while feeling like a guy who had just had sex in an ugly girl's apartment, wondering afterward how long he would have to stay without appearing to be rude. The answer was approximately ten minutes.

At one point I considered getting the guy's contact information so I could pitch a reality show like *Pawn Stars* that would involve only vintage baseball caps, but I realized I couldn't maintain a work relationship with someone I'd met only to relieve myself in his toilet.

"How did you meet this guy?" people would ask.

"Shat in his toilet," I'd reply.

The old man insisted on walking me down the two flights of stairs to the back patio of the building, where the two younger men were still sitting, nursing their beers, probably wondering if I had just been raped and at the same time not caring much.

"I want that baseball cap!" proclaimed the old man. He had earned it. I trotted back over to the show site and dug through the supply trailer until I found a red TSN cap to exchange for the man's hospitality. I ran back to the apartment building and handed it over. "Maybe I can get a shirt later too. I'll come by the show later." That sounded like trouble. I tried to appeal to him to drop it, but it was a bit difficult at this point.

Later, after the very successful show had been completed and we were seated at a tent signing autographs that we hoped would end up on beer fridges all over town, the old man kept popping his head around the corner like some sort of comic book villain. "Still waiting for that T-shirt!" he'd yell loud enough for everyone to hear, progressively drunker and drunker as the sun faded past the horizon and day turned to night. Our marketing manager, Tiffany De Groote, started to wonder why this old man was hanging around our tent the entire night and what exactly he meant when he told her, "Jay promised me a T-shirt!" I had to fess up about pooping in his apartment to her and the rest of the crew, much to their amusement and my embarrassment.

In the end, age and fatigue and a surprisingly long autograph line proved to be too much for the old man to handle, and he eventually slinked back across the road to his hats and beers. I wondered how often his family came to visit him, and if they ever dared make their way into his abode at all. I hoped that some way, somehow, I had made his day by shitting in his home, and I look forward to the day when I run into someone in New Brunswick who says, "Aren't you Jay Onrait?"

"Yes?"

"You crapped in my grandpa's toilet once!"

CHAPTER 31

The Crying Games

I KNEW THERE WAS NO WAY we'd be able to replicate the Vancouver *Olympic Morning* show at the London Games in 2012. In Vancouver, we were broadcasting at a time when there weren't actually live events going on. The whole point of our Vancouver show was to set up the events of the day ahead, recap the events of the day before, and shamelessly promote CTV personalities in a way that hadn't been done before or since. But in London, thanks to the time change, the day's events would have already begun at 6:00 a.m. EST. Suddenly, instead of waking up to us talking to drunks on Robson Street, you would be waking up to actual athletes competing in Olympic events. The Olympics! On CTV!

That meant there was little chance of rounding up the old *Olympic Morning* gang for one more go-round, not to mention the fact that CTV had made it very clear to everyone at the network that the budget would be severely scaled back from Vancouver to London. I was unsure as to whether I would be going to London at all. Okay, that's a lie. I assumed that after all the positive feedback the network had received for my Vancouver gig they would find *something* for me to do in London, but just like with *The Week That Was*, I was about to have my heart broken.

About a half-year before the Games started, we received our Olympic assignments. Mark Milliere called me at home on the day of the announcement to reveal that Dan and I would be hosting *Olympic Morning* on TSN. I was initially delighted! Then I remembered the hard truth about our coverage of the London Games; TSN hosts wouldn't be heading to London, they'd be going to Scarborough. Dan and I would be hosting from a makeshift studio at TSN in Toronto. Several play-by-play broadcasters would be calling the Games off monitors in Toronto as well. Again, this was made apparent to all of us and was not unprecedented by any stretch. The CBC had employed such a method successfully during their coverage of the Games in Turin and Beijing.

However, despite the fact that TSN was by far the most successful cable channel in the history of this country, I could not shake the unmistakable feeling that I was being demoted.

They had decided to put my friend Dave Randorf and former Canadian Olympian Catriona Le May Doan together on the London version of *Olympic Morning* on CTV instead. I completely understood the logic. Dave was an outstanding broadcaster with a ton of hosting experience on big events, and Catriona had been one of the breakout broadcasting stars of the Vancouver Games. The entire point of putting Beverly Thomson and me together for the Vancouver Games was to fill six hours of broadcast time with a bunch of different personalities under the CTV banner when there were no actual sporting events going on. My experience reading highlights came in handy for the frequent recaps during the show, and Bev's experience interviewing people from many different backgrounds was useful for the guests visiting the studio.

Now, in London, because of the time change things would

be set up much differently: The morning hosts for 2012 would be hosting a more traditional Olympic broadcast, telling viewers where they had been and then sending them to their next destination. For this reason I suppose it was deemed necessary to have a veteran broadcaster like Dave and an Olympian like Catriona as hosts to make those throws smooth and credible. This much I understood. But they were also telling Dan and me that we'd be doing the exact same show, only on TSN. So basically the Olympic Consortium executives were saying, "We know you can do this job on TSN, but we don't trust you to do it on CTV, even though you just appeared on CTV in the morning during the last Games." I felt a little like Brian Dunkleman after the first season of *American Idol*. Dunkleman co-hosted *Idol* along with Ryan Seacrest for season one, but by season two Dunkleman was gone and Seacrest began his solo quest to become the next Dick Clark.

Friends and strangers kept asking what I would be doing at the London Games. I kept lying and saying I didn't know. I hated the thought of the looks on their faces when I told them I wouldn't be doing *Olympic Morning* on CTV again. All of this was turning me into an angrier and more bitter brat than I already was. I approached my own boss, Mark Milliere, about my dissatisfaction. He made it clear there was very little he could do about the situation because he was not in charge of the Olympic Consortium. He did offer me an alternative, however, and I happily took it, even though it made me look like a bona fide jerk.

My colleague, Kate Beirness, had been working with us for just under two years at that point. Kate had been given a plum assignment for the Games, or so I thought: She was actually going to be in London for the duration, covering the Olympics for *SportsCentre*. A broadcast location would be selected somewhere in the city, and she would put together two five-minute highlight "hits" that would run every day during the Games. Frankly, it sounded awesome.

So after tiring of hearing me complain about my role, Mark finally called me at home and said, "We're sending you to London instead of Kate."

I was really, really torn. On the one hand, I was obviously elated that I would be able to attend the Games, especially on such a plum assignment. On the other hand, I felt terrible about usurping Kate this way. At least Dan would be coming along to share the blame . . .

"We're only sending you, not Dan," said Mark.

Good grief.

"Why aren't you sending Dan?" I wondered aloud to Mark.

"Not necessary," he replied. This translated to "We don't feel like spending the money."

Now I felt like a *total* douche instead of the marginal douche I'd felt like before. Their new plan was to have Dan and me host a show from 5:00 to 7:00 EST, Dan from the *SportsCentre* studios in Scarborough and me from Trafalgar Square in London. We would be linked up via satellite in a double-box format, not unlike the one Will Ferrell had enjoyed all those years ago during the 2:00 a.m. edition of *Sportsdesk*. All I knew was that I was going to be in London and not suburban Toronto for the Games, and that was good enough for me. Still, I felt like a real jackass and resented the fact that I had to stoop to this behaviour to get my ass to London.

We flew a week before the London Games were about to start. I quickly realized we very likely had the best set-up of anyone working under the Olympic Consortium banner. Our broadcast location was in Trafalgar Square in Central London, the same square that houses Canada House, the Canadian consulate in London that would be transformed into Canada Olympic House for the Games. You could literally hit it with a pitching wedge. Our actual broadcast location was a series of "sets" on a temporary scaffold occupied by us, Sky Sport Italy, Fox Digital, and CBC News Channel. The Tower of London loomed in the distance.

The Sky Sport Italy guys showed up around the same time as us, about a week before the Games. After that we didn't see them until the very end. Like the last day of the Games. I'm not even joking. The Sky Sport Italy "set" was empty the entire two and a half weeks during the London Olympics.

No one thought to provide us with a portable toilet, so at various points during the Games, I peed into Venti Starbucks cups on the Sky Sport Italia set to relieve myself after chugging a king-size energy drink and sitting in a suit for two hours. My cup overfloweth every time. Sorry, Sky Sport Italia.

Our accommodations were more than adequate (tiny but clean rooms in a central London hotel), and more importantly, a five-minute walk from work. The hotel was located in Covent Garden, an area in the centre of the city jammed with restaurants, shops, bars, and tourists on its windy streets. I had been told we would start shooting any field reports out and around the city at approximately 2:00 p.m. local time, finishing around 5:00. That gave me a couple of hours to get ready and grab a quick dinner, write the show around 7:00 p.m., host from 10:00 to midnight, and then fix up any mistakes for the morning show segments until 12:30 a.m.

It was, in my mind, possibly the greatest Olympic broadcast schedule ever. I would be able to go out with the crew after every show, albeit not to pubs, as they all closed down at midnight. None of us understood why the pubs closed so early until we realized everyone in London started drinking at 4:00 p.m. and was pretty much obliterated by 8:00. Luckily, we discovered that in London the hotel bars are there to serve the hotel guests. If the hotel guests want to stay up and drink until 5:00 a.m. every single night, then the hotel bar will stay open until 5:00 a.m. every single night. Not surprisingly, our hotel bar was open until 5:00 a.m. every single night.

The next day we rehearsed our first show from Trafalgar Square. Dean Willers, our veteran camera guy, was also serving as lighting director, floor director, set decorator, assistant sound engineer, and continuity person. In other words, a typical Canadian television shoot. At one point Olympic Consortium executives sent us an e-mail congratulating us on the look of our shows and thanking "the crew" for their hard work. Dean really enjoyed that line. "Tell them the crew appreciates it," he said.

That night we had managed to convince Leigh, the manager of the Maple Leaf Pub in the heart of Covent Garden, to stay open a bit later for us so we could celebrate our first broadcast. Leigh, like almost all the employees at the Maple Leaf, was Canadian. A former student from Vancouver who'd come over to Europe to travel, she had run out of money and gotten a job at the only Canadian pub in London to make ends meet, only to find herself still living in the city and still working at the pub two years later.

I had visited the Maple Leaf years earlier during the aforementioned backpacking trip of 1998. In fact, I was there on July 1, 1998, because I assumed it would be a big Canada Day party, and for once in my life I had made a correct assumption. The evening ended with the entire bar singing "Summer of '69." I had hoped to replicate that experience at one point during these Games for a feature story, but tonight was all about celebrating our successful first broadcast. Six of us gathered around the table drinking Sleeman beer and downing tequila shots until Leigh finally kicked us out around 3:00 a.m. In an incredible stroke of luck, the pub was just around the corner from our hotel. I managed to make it all the way back to my room, tear off my suit and shoes, and fall into bed.

About an hour later, I was awaked by the sound of someone puking. That someone was me.

I had literally woken myself up by vomiting uncontrollably all over myself and all over the bed sheets. It says something about my state of mind during that moment that I paid it no attention and immediately went back to sleep. Luckily, I was sort of propped up on my pillow so there was no danger of choking on my own vomit like Bon Scott or John Bonham.

Deep into another slumber, I was awakened again about an hour later when I heard a loud, piercing wail that sounded like my smoke detector back home. I strained my eyes to look straight up at the ceiling: Sure enough, there was a smoke detector in my room, and I had now determined that it was somehow going off at full volume and likely waking up the entire hotel, or at the very least my entire floor. I didn't stop to think about why my smoke detector might have been going off. I just wanted the sound to end so I could go back to sleep.

I barely managed to pull myself out of my puke-stained bed, naked except for my Calvin Klein boxer briefs, eyes straining to adjust to the light. I tried desperately to find a button that might shut off the smoke detector before the hotel manager came up to my room. The sound of the siren was so loud, so piercing, that surely other guests had started to stream out of their rooms to figure out what was going on. I quickly gave up trying to find an off button and ripped the cover off the smoke detector in hopes of taking out the battery. But after I tore out the battery the piercing wail persisted. I was at a loss. I was also still drunk and half asleep. Why wouldn't this damn smoke detector turn off? Finally I gave up and accepted my fate: I would likely have to find another hotel after this incident. But that daunting prospect paled in comparison to the appeal of simply falling back on my sick-stained sheets and returning to a drunken slumber. I was very likely in deep trouble, but it was nothing I couldn't put off until the light of day.

The next day I woke late for a mandatory security meeting at the International Broadcast Centre at the Olympic Park in East London. There was no time to assess the disastrous situation from the evening before. I showered the vomit off my body and gathered the sheets in a pile, surrounding the worst-stained sheets with the ones that were still relatively clean in hopes the maid might just gather them up that way and not notice the mess I had made. I noticed a tiny vomit stain on the mattress itself but hoped the cleaning staff might not notice, as the stain was about the size of a toonie (a Canadian two-dollar coin, for all you international readers). I didn't even have the time or the sense to replace the cover on the smoke detector. I figured the maids would replace it, so I left them a five-pound tip in hopes of them just returning the room to normal and keeping things quiet. I should have left a twenty-pound tip.

I met the rest of the crew, and as we prepared to leave for the shoot, one of our camera guys, Dave Parker, asked why I hadn't ended up in the lobby last night.

"Why would I have ended up in the lobby?" I wondered.

"Because of the fire alarm?" said Dave with a look on his face that said "Are you really that dumb?"

I am really that dumb.

"How could you *not* hear it? There were old people in pajamas coming down the stairwell. I grabbed my camera, came down to the lobby, and started shooting footage," said Dave.

It all became clear. In my fall-down, puke-riddled, drunken stupor, I had mistaken an ear-splitting alarm in a massive ten-storey hotel for the sound of a regular, tiny smoke detector. That would of course explain why the alarm continued after I took the batteries out of the detector. Basically, the moral of the story is I am an idiot. Still, I laughed it off. I just hoped the maids would clean the sheets and we could all forget this incident had ever happened.

After returning to the room following the meeting, I found a letter waiting for me under the door:

Guest Name: Mr. Jay Onrait
Arrival Date: 20/07/2012
Departure Date: 13/08/2012

Room: 846
Saturday, 21 July 2012

Dear Mr. Onrait,
  Thank you so much for choosing the ███████████
Hotel in London. I hope that you are having a relaxed and
pleasant stay with us.
  It has been brought to my attention that there was
traces of vomit in your room, namely in your bed, which
have caused damage to the duvet, the bed linens and the
pillowcases.
  I have also been informed that the smoke detector has
been removed from its place. May I reiterate that since July
2007 our hotel is Smoke Free; it is against the law to smoke
in any part of the hotel, including guest bedrooms and pub-
lic areas. It is also against the law to tamper or remove any
of the fire prevention equipment.
  We have collected photographic evidence and we are
now assessing the cost of cleaning the room and replacing
the damaged items. The costs for the cleaning and replacing
the damaged items will be communicated to you on
Monday.
  Kind Regards,
  ███████████
  Duty Manager

Looks like I *really* did not leave a big enough tip.

Now I was in trouble. They thought I had removed the cover off
the smoke detector because I was smoking in my room. I quickly
realized that my only real defence in this case was pure stupidity.

Would the duty manager really believe that the reason I had
torn the cover off his smoke detector in the middle of the night was

because I thought the loud piercing sound of the hotel fire alarm was actually my smoke detector? Even though it was the truth, it sounded completely ridiculous even to me. Surely, however, they wouldn't charge me for the soiled sheets. How hard is it to get vomit out of sheets? Think of all the bodily fluids that are soaked into the sheet fibres of every hotel you've ever been to. This was downtown London for God's sake! There was no way in *hell* I was the first person to fill my own hotel room bed with the contents of my stomach. I was confident that after apologizing in person I would be charged a very small fee, and life at the hotel would continue unabated.

Two days later I received another letter under my door:

Guest Name: Mr. Jay Onrait
Arrival Date: 20/07/2012
Departure Date: 13/08/2012
Room: 846
Monday, 23 July 2012

Dear Mr. Onrait,
Thank you so much for choosing the ▮▮▮▮▮▮▮▮
Hotel in London. I hope that you are having a relaxed and pleasant stay with us.

Following the previous letter sent to you I am writing to inform you about the charges you will incur. We will be applying a charge of 120.00 pounds that will be added to your room bill.

The reason for this charge is explained below:
120.00 – Cost of replacing the mattress
You can come to the reception to settle this amount at your earliest convenience.

Mr. Onrait, if you require any further assistance please do not hesitate to contact me.

Kind regards,

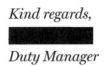

Duty Manager

Well, this was a problem. One hundred twenty pounds? There was *no way* I was paying that much for soiled sheets. I also knew there was *no way* the hotel was going to replace that mattress. It was clear from the incident that I was a dumb, dumb man, but I was no pushover. I vowed to fight it.

The next day I was awakened by the sounds of construction workers outside my window. Turns out they were doing work on the roof of the hotel, and they had decided to start at the ungodly hour of 8:00 a.m. *Unacceptable!* I thought to myself. I also saw it as an opportunity. This was my way of getting out of paying that bill.

I called down to the duty manager and apologized for trashing his room like Charlie Sheen, and then I promptly launched into a complaint about the construction noise. I told him I was working late throughout the Games (true, but not *that* late). I then informed him that the construction had in fact ruined my entire workday, and as such, I should not be held accountable for the damage I had done to the room on the 21st of July. This seemed like a stretch but also a plausible way to get out of paying the hotel almost 300 Canadian dollars. He apologized for the noise and promised to take it into consideration.

Two days later, another letter under my door:

Mr. Jay Onrait
Room 846
c/o 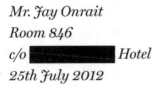 *Hotel*
25th July 2012

Dear Mr. Onrait,

I acknowledge receipt of your complaint made to ▓▓▓▓▓▓▓▓*, Duty Manager, regarding a charge of 120.00 added to your account.*

I have now had the opportunity to investigate the matter and am in a position to inform you that, on Saturday 21st July, Housekeeping Department brought to the Duty Manager's attention that there were body fluids all over the bed and that the fire detector has been disabled.

May I bring to your attention that, as per the photographic evidence, the following linen have been badly stained and discarded: pillows, pillowcases, duvet, duvet cover, bottom sheet, mattress protector. Pillows, duvets and mattress protectors are made with fire retardant fabrics and for heavy use, hence, the cost to replace them is higher.

I would like to inform you that, when the linen is seriously tarnished by body fluids, the linen is thrown away and replaced. It is very well known that body fluids could contain bacteria, gastric acid, blood and other liquids which are Health hazards for the staff handling the items stained.

I comprehend that you consider the amount of 120.00 being exaggerated, but as per the above explanation you will understand the reasons why.

I will not make any comments on the subject of the smoke detector being de-activated and the significance of it, as I understand you have apologized to ▓▓▓▓▓▓ *the day after the event occurred.*

Finally, in relation to the noise complaint made yesterday, regrettable, an external contractor did not realize that they should have not carried out works in the early hours. The contractors were summoned to stop the noise immedi-

ately. Nevertheless, we did not receive any other complaint in relation to this matter.

Mr. Onrait, I do hope that the rest of your stay is an enjoyable and relaxing one and if you require any assistance, please do not hesitate to contact the Duty Manager who will be more than delighted to offer their help.

Yours sincerely,

███████████████

Operations Manager

I was screwed.

I decided to drop the fight, for now at least. Maybe they would forget about it.

CHAPTER 32

Have You Seen This Dan?

THE FIRST THREE SHOWS WE DID from Trafalgar Square went incredibly well. No major delays in the feed from Toronto, so there weren't any new awkwardly long pauses while we chatted via satellite, just the normal awkwardly long pauses that we usually have on the show.

Since Dan wasn't at the Games, I had come up with a "game show" idea to feature him as prominently as possible. I had our marketing manager, Tiffany De Groote, create a couple of T-shirts for me to wear with a giant picture of Dan's face. The plan was to corner Olympic athletes and broadcasters from countries other than Canada and have them play the breakout hit game show of the London Olympics, "Have You Seen This Dan?" Guests would try to identity the Dan on the front of my T-shirt in a multiple choice question.

We made our way down to the NBC Olympic cafeteria at the International Broadcast Centre to try to round up some popular NBC personalities for the segment. Imagine my surprise when the first NBC star I ran into was none other than *American Idol* host Ryan Seacrest! He was so tiny I wanted to put him in my pocket! Not just short, but skinny. He honestly had the body of a thirteen-year-old girl whose boobs hadn't developed. But what a nice gentleman he was when I approached him out of nowhere.

"Ryan, Jay Onrait from *SportsCentre* in Canada. Want to do a quick interview with us and guess who the famous Canadian is on this T-shirt?" I asked him as he tried to make his way into the NBC cafeteria, probably to eat a single grape.

"Sure!" said Seacrest. Even I was surprised by how gung-ho he seemed. What a great guy! My camera guy, Dean Willers, was about to turn on his camera when suddenly two thirty-something women dressed in identical cardigans with identical necklaces closed Seacrest off like a castle shutting its gates.

"No! He can't do it, sorry. He's too busy." It was his duo of publicists. They were in charge of booking interviews for him, and obviously I hadn't gone through the proper channels. In our business these days that's a no-no. It's certainly understandable. We have great publicists at TSN who book our interviews and separate the legit interviewers from the guys who are just trying to make us look dumber than we already are and waste our time. I am certainly happy that we have publicists do that for us. But in this case I thought Seacrest's publicists were going a bit too far. Seacrest was clearly ready to do the interview, I had full Olympic credentials hanging around my neck, and the entire thing would have taken approximately one minute. Instead, Seacrest walked away with shrugged shoulders and a sheepish look that said, "Sorry, dude, you know how this works." I'll never forget how nice he was, though, and I'll never forget how mean his two publicists were.

We ended up getting Craig Sager from *NBA on TNT* to join us for a "Have You Seen This Dan?" segment, as well as Jim Gray from NBC Sports and one of my personal favourite sportscasters ever and a huge influence on my career, Dan Patrick. It was Dan who memorably teamed up with Keith Olbermann in the mid-1990s to form what is universally regarded as the greatest highlight show anchor duo in the history of sports broadcasting. Dan left ESPN and was now hosting a syndicated radio show that we carried on TSN Radio across the country. He was in London covering the Olympics for NBC because he was also the host of the *Football Night in America* highlight show that aired just before the Sunday night NFL game on NBC. The Sunday nighter and *Football Night in America* also aired on TSN. I joked with him at the start of the segment that he was on TSN more than I was. He laughed and then made fun of my haircut. At that very moment I really loved my job.

Early on in the Games, we received an e-mail from a publicity agency representing German tennis legend Boris Becker. Would we be interested in interviewing Mr. Becker about his new role as an ambassador for English tourism? Turns out the three-time Wimbledon winner had moved to London years ago and had now been hired for a Travel Britain advertisement campaign. Normally, we would stay far, far away from this so-called press conference, which would really be nothing more than an extended in-person commercial. Unfortunately, we were having no luck booking broadcasters through NBC's publicity department; in fact, NBC's publicity department was completely ignoring our e-mails, denying us access to their talent. Becker was someone all Canadian sports fans would recognize, and this seemed like a good opportunity to play another rousing game of "Have You Seen This Dan?" with a participant who would genuinely have no idea who the man on the front of my T-shirt was. Becker was also one of my all-time favourite athletes, and the opportunity to interview him one-on-one, regardless of the reason, was simply too good to pass up. I was always a Becker guy and couldn't understand why anyone would be an Edberg guy.

Dean and I made our way to a posh hotel about ten minutes

from Trafalgar Square, where a surprisingly large group of local and international media had gathered to talk to Becker about his new endeavour. Becker walked into the room wearing a not-too-trendy suit and button-up shirt, no tie, but it was his face that really caught my eye. His fair skin was bright red, and he looked *extremely* puffy, with big bags under his eyes. He was unshaven. His was the face of a man who had been drinking heavily the night before and probably wanted to be anywhere but this hotel right now. I suddenly realized he might not be in the mood to guess the identity of some random Canadian on some random Canadian's T-shirt.

After Becker was introduced, we were all subjected to his new commercial, which was surprisingly tasteful and well done, followed by a pre-selected interviewer asking him a series of standard questions about his new Travel Britain role. After another half-hour or so, the interviewer turned to us seated in front of him and opened things up to the floor for questions. The first two were innocent enough, pretty much verbatim from what the one-on-one interviewer had already asked him, but the third interviewer was different. She had travelled to the event all the way from Germany and asked her question first in German and then in English:

"Mr. Becker, I'm wondering if you have considered how German people might feel about you, being one of the world's most famous German people, endorsing a campaign to travel to Britain. Do you think that the German people will be disappointed that you didn't elect to do a similar campaign in your home country instead?"

On the surface, Becker didn't seem fazed by the question. Instead, he answered in a measured and thoughtful way in German and then English so we could all understand. He then carried on to the next question. Maybe Boris wasn't in such a bad mood after all. *Maybe this whole day would work out okay*, I thought to myself.

After the press questions had been exhausted, those of us who wanted to go one-on-one with the tennis star were corralled into a corner just outside of the conference room. As I found my place in line, I saw the German reporter and two of her colleagues gather just outside the room, speaking quietly among themselves. Suddenly, Boris came flying out of the room toward them, followed by his own press agent, who seemed to be trying to calm him down. Boris approached the German reporter and her colleagues and began berating them in their native tongue. Speaking quickly and sternly but not shouting, never raising his voice, it was clear to me and *everyone* in the room he was unhappy with the question she had asked and was going to let her know about it. You didn't even need to understand a speck of *Deutsch* to understand that the former Olympic gold medallist was upset. His rant toward the reporter lasted about thirty seconds, after which she turned toward us. The German reporter's face was white. I thought she might start to cry.

At that point it was almost my turn to interview him, and quite frankly, I was now shitting myself.

I was up after a stunning English girl who was strictly told by Becker's PR agent that she was allowed a total of two questions and then she had to move on. Five questions later it was my turn. I walked up to Boris, who smiled amiably and shook my hand. His was the pungent smell of stale booze, cigarettes, and regret.

I quickly explained the situation: "This is a famous Canadian named Dan on my T-shirt. Can you guess which Canadian Dan it is?"

Often, when you go to a press conference like this, whether it's for a film or a television show or a new condo some celebrity is endorsing, the celebrity has been asked the same question over and over and over. This situation was no different. Pretty much everyone here was asking the same first question: Why did you decide to endorse Travel Britain? For some the name of the game is politely answering these same questions over and over as quickly as possible, fulfilling their obligation, and getting the fuck out of there. So when you throw a curveball into the mix like I was doing with my "game show," you are entering into a serious risk/reward situation. There will be no middle ground. Either the subject will be delighted to not have to answer the same questions he or she has just answered a million times and will participate with unbridled enthusiasm, *or* the subject will be annoyed that you tried to go "off script," telling you to get on with it and stop wasting valuable time, and you'll slink away full of shame. Basically I was in the same conundrum I faced when presenting Will Ferrell with that piece of hotel stationery. Based on Boris's reaction to the inquiry from the German woman, I was fearing the worst.

But Boris was delighted.

His face lit up like a tannenbaum. "What is this?" he asked with genuine curiosity and delight.

"Oh, just a fun little game from Canada!" I replied with genuine relief in my voice. Becker was *in*. I started to lay out the multiple choice questions for him.

"Boris Becker . . . Is this [gesturing to my T-shirt] . . . the father of Canadian tennis star Milos Raonic, *Dan* Raonic?"

Boris smiled, he was enjoying this. He had forgotten all about the woman who dared question his loyalty to his own country.

"Is it . . . the brother of Canadian superstar vocalist Celine Dion, *Dan* Dion?"

Boris looked into the camera with a goofy face that said "I don't know what's happening but I like it!"

"Is it . . . famous Canadian sports anchor Dan O'Toole? *Or* . . . is it famous Canadian radio personality Tarzan Dan? Boris . . . HAVE YOU SEEN THIS DAN?"

Boris studied the face on my T-shirt again. He concluded that it was not "the father of Raonic" and ultimately decided it must be Tarzan Dan. I shook my head. "Well, who *is* it?" he demanded. He wanted the answer to this age-old question as much as anyone. I informed him that the man on my shirt was, in fact, a "famous"

Canadian sportscaster, and he seemed satisfied. Boris thanked me for my time, made sure to let me know there was a catered lunch available to me, shook my hand, and bid me *Auf Wiedersehen*.

My next venture out and about in London would not end with such good vibes.

CHAPTER 33

The Mexicans

OVERALL, OUR FIRST FEW SHOWS from Trafalgar Square were going well, which is why I was so surprised when Ken called me one afternoon before we were about to shoot our fourth show: "How would you feel about Dan coming over to London?"

I was shocked and delighted. TSN was never known for spending money on production if they didn't have to, especially when it was clear the shows were working and there were no technical issues. Instead, Ken explained that he simply thought the show would be better if Dan were in London and not via satellite in a studio. I couldn't have agreed more. As technically flawless as the shows were, there was a noticeable and understandable drop-off in energy when we would cut from a solo shot of me in Trafalgar Square with its many sirens back to the Scarborough studio, which was designed to cut out excess newsroom noise. Plus, I just think I'm better with a co-host. A little of me goes a long way.

Ken explained that Dan would be flying over tomorrow and would start co-hosting with me the next day. I immediately e-mailed

Dan and got his thoughts. He was obviously thrilled, as he had never been to Europe before. The catch was that Nicole Anderson, our production manager, would not be able to get Dan credentials for any Olympic events because that was a process you needed to apply for months in advance. I knew full well Dan wouldn't care. Would he have loved to go to Olympic events? Absolutely. But given the choice between going to London for three weeks with no access to events and staying in Scarborough with access only to the Jack Astor's restaurant across the street, Dan wisely agreed to the flight across the pond. He ended up spending all of his mornings in London shopping for gifts for his wife and daughters and buying shoes for himself. I think he bought a different pair of shoes every single day of the Games. He was like a young Imelda Marcos those two weeks.

⚡

All the broadcasters working for the Olympic Consortium were fortunate enough to be assigned drivers who took us from one corner of this massive city to another. In Vancouver, many of these drivers were volunteers who simply wanted to be a part of the Olympic festivities. All well and good, except some of them had a better grasp of the Vancouver streets than others. In London, they opted for a simpler and more effective method of transporting broadcasters around: retired volunteer police officers. Talk about a group of guys who knew the city streets and the best way to get around them. We were lucky enough to be assigned a retired officer named Ian Taylor. Ian ended up being one of my favourite people of the entire trip. Every time we would hop into his car to be driven from the hotel to the Olympic Park in the East End of London, we would learn something new about Britain, the Royal Family, and the English people in general. I found him fascinating and loved hearing his stories about the Thatcher years, the Blair years, and how things had changed now with David Cameron at the helm. He was a true English gentleman, and he was also unafraid of taking the piss out of us at all times. As Ian liked to say, "I'm a bloody pensioner! I couldn't give a fuck about you lot!"

Nicole sent Ian to pick up Dan at Heathrow Airport and had him wear one of the T-shirts with a giant picture of Dan's face on it. That was the first thing Dan saw when he went to collect his luggage, and of course he was delighted. He started hosting with me from Trafalgar Square right away, and the shows were instantly more fun.

Trafalgar Square was a dream location to broadcast from for several reasons. It was completely central, with plenty of people milling about during the day, so we could complete our daily rendition of "God Save the Queen" with a large group of English folk. It was TSN VP Ken Volden's idea to end each show with the national anthem of the host country. He had apparently seen it done by an anchor team during the Sydney Olympics in Australia. What he didn't mention was that the anchor team he was referring to was probably out of the business by this point, or in jail.

There was only one problem with Trafalgar Square: It essentially closed down at night. We were under the impression it would be more like Vancouver, where Robson Square was packed until midnight or later every evening during the Winter Games. But Trafalgar Square didn't even have big screens showing Olympic events, and by around 10:00 p.m. local time, the square started to thin out so that all we were left with as a background audience were a *lot* of drunks, a few families out too late, and a smattering of couples and recent hookups unashamed about some serious PDA. I have never been to a city where the citizens were so willing to drunkenly make out next to a fountain, the cops standing by watching with a look of serious disinterest on their faces.

Dan and I thought maybe we'd be able to get the crowd involved in highlights and "bits" in much the same way we do every year on the Kraft Tour. When Ken Volden told us he wanted to end every show with "God Save the Queen," I imagined a scene right out of Glastonbury, with a huge crowd belting out the words and trying to top each other every night. But since the crowd averaged about seven people a night, that wasn't going to be possible.

Instead, we would venture out with camera guy Dean during the day. We could have just filmed the segment in Trafalgar Square every day, which was packed during daylight hours, but we did our best to make an effort to switch things up as much as possible: We gathered a crowd exiting the beach volleyball venue, and we corralled huge groups of Olympic Park attendees. For one show we gathered a small group of Olympic volunteers watching Canada's women's gymnastics team compete at the O2 Arena. Then one day we simply forgot to do it. We had started to write the show, and suddenly I jumped up and screamed, "We forgot to do 'God Save the Queen'!"

"I guess we just don't have it for tonight's show, then," said Dean, who had already set up his camera and lights to film our show and wasn't pleased at the idea of tearing everything down and having to put it back up again.

"We can do this. Dan, let's go!" We were on a mission: round up as many Brits as we possibly could among the stragglers, drunks, and general ne'er-do-wells that filled the square. It was still relatively early, so we still had a chance to make the segment look good. But there was one major impediment . . .

The Mexicans.

Mexico ended up having a pretty successful Olympics. Their

always competitive men's soccer team upset Brazil for the gold medal, resulting in easily the loudest and craziest crowd behind us in Trafalgar Square. We had also seen smaller but still boisterous groups of Mexicans in the square before that men's soccer final, and tonight was no different. Turns out Mexico was becoming a nation of divers, and that particular evening one of their divers had captured a bronze. A crowd of about a hundred Mexicans and Mexican-Britons had gathered to celebrate, and they brought libations. We loved to hang over our scaffolding and listen to them sing celebratory songs until they eventually got tired or too drunk and went home. Tonight, however, we would be getting to know them more intimately.

Me, Dan, and our English broadcast intern Charlotte made our way into the square to try to round up English people to sing and get this whole exercise over with as quickly as possible. We were approaching people at the worst possible time, as everyone was on their way to dinner or had just spent the entire day in the square. No one was interested in sticking around to sing. We finally rounded up a nice young English family and two English women around thirty years old who were dressed like Olympic torches, complete with Union Jack–coloured flames shooting out from their foreheads. But that's all we had, and suddenly we were desperate. Maybe that's why we didn't object when the Mexican fans spotted us, asked us what we were doing, and promptly plunked themselves right in front of our camera to join in the festivities.

This would ordinarily have been wonderful, but there was one key issue: Almost none of them spoke English. At least they pretended not to, so it was tricky trying to explain exactly what was going on, much less get them to co-operate. Two of the younger females in their group became their de facto spokespeople by virtue of their understanding of the Queen's language; but the rest of the group, fuelled by their country's Olympic victory and a large quantity of what appeared to be decent tequila, were not in the mood to be cor-ralled for a television segment. They were not in the mood to learn the words to the Queen's anthem either. It was up to me, the young English family, the two English girls, and Dan to drown them out. There was simply no stopping it, and so we rolled tape and hoped for the best.

When it was all over, the look of disgust on our camera guy's face was something I will never forget. Dean was a man used to carefully organized and constructed television shots that were lit and arranged beautifully and carefully. Instead, he got what looked like the mosh pit at Lollapalooza 1993. Mexicans jostling with each other. The English family just trying to protect their kids from get-ting tequila poured on their heads. The two English girls rejecting the advances of drunken louts and clearly regretting having run into us at all. The entire thing was a debacle, but I thought it really evoked the Olympic spirit of nations coming together for one com-mon goal. Our retired English police officer, Ian, described the entire scene by using his favourite new North American slang term that we had taught him the day before:

"It was a *clusterfuck*."

CHAPTER 34

The Battle for 221B Baker Street

OUR PRODUCTION MANAGER, Nicole Anderson, had found a wonderful costume shop in London and had started to source out some great outfits. She ended up going with two classics: an old-time "London bobby" police officer and a pretty authentic Sherlock Holmes outfit. There was no rhyme nor reason to choosing either of these costumes for use on our show. We were simply trying to get the most English stuff into the show as possible.

First, we decided to use the London bobby costume. It was so simple. I dressed up in the full gear and ended up finding a bobby officer helmet at a corner store. Plastic, cheap, perfect. Carol, our English makeup artist, kindly provided me with some moustache glue and I applied a pretty thick fake duster under my nose. Normally, I needed only a month to grow a beautiful soup strainer, but we didn't have that kind of time right now—the fake one would have to do. Unfortunately, I tend to sweat right above my upper lip, and the 'stache kept falling off my face and onto the ground. No matter.

Dean set up his camera in Trafalgar Square in the middle of the day when tons of people were wandering around and lining up to get into the National Gallery. Real police officers were everywhere. I wandered up to them in my outfit and proceeded to make small talk. Dean had outfitted me with a small microphone that picked up every word of our conversation. The real cops were on to me quickly, but they played along nicely. I spent the rest of the shoot wandering around the square and pretending to help tourists. I even ran into a pair of Buddhist monks. The entire shoot was completed without incident and proved to be a big hit.

Then there was Sherlock Holmes.

The idea was to put on the Holmes outfit, hop into the car with Ian, and have him drive us to Sherlock Holmes's address: 221B Baker Street. It was about a fifteen-minute drive from Trafalgar Square in central London with all the traffic. We hoped to simply get some shots of me wandering around Sherlock's address, and that was honestly about it. As I said, none of these shoots were elaborately planned. We hoped to get in and out of there without much trouble. Instead, the exact opposite happened.

When we pulled up to 221B Baker Street, we noticed that someone had had the foresight to build a Sherlock Holmes Museum there. Standing right at the doorway of the famous address was a tall chap like myself dressed in full Sherlock Holmes gear. Though we may have been biased, Dean, Ian, and I all agreed that my rented Sherlock costume was actually better than the one the official museum Holmes was sporting. After we cased the joint for a few minutes from our car, the museum Sherlock wandered inside, likely to relieve himself after a busy morning spent taking pictures with tourists.

We quickly sprang into action: Dean set the camera up right in front of the doorway of 221B and I stood in front of it with my plastic pipe, making very serious and pensive detective faces. That should have been it. We should have peeled out of there and been done with the place. But suddenly I was the centre of attention. All of the tourists standing around waiting to get pictures with Sherlock Holmes now thought I was the Holmes hired by the museum. Suddenly, I had a lineup of people standing by with their iPhones and cameras wanting to get a picture with Sherlock. I gamely played along, and Dean continued to roll camera on the entire thing. Surely we could use this material. I might have just stayed there all day until I felt a hand in the small of my back nudge me forward, and a condescending voice behind me said, "I'm going to need you to get off these steps, please."

It was the other Sherlock.

He had a smug and unimpressed look on his face. There was anger in his voice. I had stepped into his tiny spotlight, taken away the one thing in his life that gave him joy, and he was not happy about it. I conceded the step to him and directed the tourists to start taking pictures with the "real" Sherlock. We had pretty much all the material we needed for the shoot anyway. Dean continued to get shots of the exterior of the building for cover purposes. I wandered back on the sidewalk, but the tourists continued to flock toward me and away from the "real" Sherlock. It was beyond my control, and I wasn't about to stop taking pictures with people when they had come all this way to get pictures with Sherlock Holmes. The "real" Sherlock was clearly unimpressed that he was no longer the star of the show. All this was delighting me to no end.

Once Dean had indicated he was finished shooting, he gathered his camera and I grabbed his tripod. I just realized that sounds dirty. I did not grab his penis. I grabbed the actual tripod that he used to host his camera in one place. We started to make our way back to Ian's car, walking past the "real" Sherlock one last time. I simply could not resist.

As I walked by, he looked up at me, and I flipped him the bird.

Gave him the finger. Whatever you want to call it. I really felt he deserved it after the way he had treated us that day, but I wanted to be subtle, didn't want to cause a scene. I thought I had made my point and life would continue on.

But the "real" Sherlock had other ideas.

We walked across the street, and Dean took some more shots of me wandering around in my Holmes outfit. We then declared ourselves done and set the camera up next to the car so we could look into Dean's camera monitor; he played back the footage he had just shot so we could make sure we had everything we needed before we took off back to our little temporary office in Trafalgar Square. Dean and I were both peering into the monitor and commenting on the stuff he had shot. I looked up for some reason and saw a man near the Holmes museum about thirty feet away. He pointed in my direction and started walking toward me with purpose. I looked behind me. Was he pointing at me? He looked to be a normal guy in a white shirt and black trousers. All of a sudden he was right in front of me.

"Flip me the bird, will you!" he screamed while reaching back and trying to deliver what I can only describe as a "slap" toward my face. Imagine during Shakespearean times when English gentlemen would duel each other by slapping each other with their gloves. That was pretty much what this guy tried with me, except without gloves. I managed to lean back in a nonchalant way and avoid the blow. He had removed his costume and was now ready to fight me over the fact that I had given him the finger. The finger! In North America, motorists give each other the finger every 1.3 seconds. It's practically like waving at this point. When I finally realized what was going on, I started laughing.

Dean and Ian quickly stepped in between us, to his objection: "Standing behind your tough friends, eh?" he screamed. I was disappointed. Why hadn't he just left his Holmes outfit on? Imagine how much funnier this would be to onlookers if two guys dressed as Sherlock Holmes started fighting in front of the Sherlock Holmes museum? It would have been a true Borat moment. Amazingly, two London police officers were standing nearby watching the entire thing, and they grabbed the "real" Holmes and dragged him away to calm him down. The three of us looked at each other in disbelief. Had that really just happened? Had I just been "slap-attacked" by a man who was likely a frustrated actor trying to make ends meet by working at a cheesy museum? Indeed I had. The Olympics!

⚡

That night we encountered no trouble whatsoever at legendary jazz club Ronnie Scott's, a Soho institution we frequented throughout the Games, listening to jazz and quietly talking about that evening's show while drinking double gin and tonics. We managed to squeeze into a booth and proceeded to get drunk. Young British couples were snogging in booths near us. Local players would finish the night, and I was always amazed how young they were and that young people were still so passionate about jazz. It made me feel good.

After the bar closed, we all hopped into rickshaws and raced back to our hotel, where we closed down the lobby bar. We ordered chicken tikka masala and several rounds of *double* double gin and tonics and a few shots of tequila and then charged the entire bill to TSN reporter Brent Wallace's room because Brent never came out with us. The night continued until there were only three of us sitting in the lobby, absolutely wasted, when CTV lighting director Slobodan Marin walked in through the front door at 5:00 a.m. after his overnight shift of Brian Williams's CTV *Olympic Prime Time* show.

"Do you want to come with me to see the Dream Team play tomorrow?" he asked.

Without thinking I said yes immediately. Of course I wanted to see Kobe, LeBron, and the best U.S. basketball players beat up on some unfortunate Eastern European country. I crashed and grabbed a few hours of sleep, and then I woke up and met Slobo in the lobby. He looked absolutely shocked to see me.

"Oh! You're a tough guy!" he said. I think he was being serious.

"I'm not feeling great, but I'm a man of my word!" I lied. I honestly had no idea how I'd managed to wake up and make it down to the lobby at this hour.

"You know what my dad used to say when I was growing up in Serbia and I started going out to bars with my friends and staying up all night?"

I waited intently . . .

"If you're going to be a man at night, you'd better be a man in the morning."

CHAPTER 35

Our Makeup Artist Nearly Dies

We watched the closing ceremony at Canada House in Trafalgar Square. I really wanted to grab scalper tickets and see Blur at Hyde Park in what was purported to be their last ever show, but I figured it didn't make much sense for me to take off by myself and see a concert I didn't even have tickets for. Plus, no one else was interested in going. I wasn't too heartbroken at the time. I figured after the past three weeks it was only appropriate I go out and get drunk with the gang who had gone through all this madness with me; I didn't want to be an anti-social weirdo. Turns out I should have been an anti-social weirdo. That night might have turned out much better than it did.

Carol, our makeup artist, was one of the most posh people I had ever met. Proper language, great taste in restaurants, and well connected. She told us of barbeques on weekends that she would attend. I imagined they featured a number of different types of cucumber salads on a beautifully decorated garden table, with plenty of society talk. She was Bill and Melinda Gates's personal makeup artist whenever they travelled to Europe for charity work. She had worked extensively in film and television. In fact, it seemed as if she was slumming it a bit working for a Canadian sports network during these Games. She was a lovely lady and she immediately seemed to take a shine to Dean, our camera operator, who was equally kind to her and tried to make her feel welcome. Each night we hosted the "Olympic Suppertime Spectacular," it would be Dan and me on the desk, Dean behind the camera, and Carol in a chair nearby, ready to do makeup touch-ups whenever needed. She laughed at all our jokes and sketches. It was a great little group.

After we finished the final show on the Trafalgar Square set, the entire crew headed to Canada House. Molson representatives had been present throughout the Games, even bringing over the occasional case of beer to the set and allowing us to borrow ice from them to keep our energy drinks cold. The evening of the closing ceremony, the Molson Canadian was flowing freely and so was the red and white wine. It was a blast watching the ceremony with a room full of Canadians, no major celebrities unless you count the twins from *Property Brothers*, who were actually flooded with requests for pictures. I approached them for a picture since my mom is a fan. They had absolutely no idea who I was.

After the Spice Girls appeared on TV to what was easily the loudest ovation of the night, the crowd started to thin out a bit, and most of our crew decided to make their way across the city to attend the CTV Olympic Consortium wrap party. I stayed behind with Dan and Carol. At one point toward the end of the ceremony the three of us sat in front of a huge plasma screen watching Roger Daltrey and Pete Townshend play a few Who hits. Dan excused himself to use the washroom, and I leaned over to Carol and said, "Roger Daltrey's voice still sounds great, doesn't it?" expecting her to wax poetic about her love of the English band. But Carol didn't have a response. It's not that she didn't have anything to say about the subject matter, she just literally did not respond. I paid it no attention, figuring she was just tired.

Thirty seconds later Carol stood up, and before I could take my eyes off the screen to see what was happening, she teetered in one spot for a half-second before tipping forward and falling flat on her face with an enormous THUMP. She did this in front of 300 people. Time stood still. I was horrified. How had I not seen how drunk she was. Did she have a concussion? Was she dead?

No time to lament past decisions. I fell down on my knees as she slowly turned over. She was awake, but barely. A crowd of horrified Canadians had gathered at that point, every one of them probably wishing they hadn't invited the TSN people to their closing cere-mony party. Thankfully, because so many athletes were on hand, plenty of trainers and sports medicine people were there too. There was also a doctor from Surrey, B.C., who was attending the Olympics with his family while volunteering at Canada House. Thankfully, Carol would get the care she needed. I know you're reading this and thinking that the only "care" Carol needed was sleep, water, and half a bottle of Advil, but I was genuinely paranoid about the possibility she might have a concussion after that head-slam.

The doctor and two sports medicine people carefully helped her to a chair and kept her there for the next hour and a half, ask-ing her questions about her whereabouts, who she was, whether she had someone waiting for her at home, and so on. The whole thing was pretty shocking, to be honest. I had no idea she had consumed that much alcohol. Later, during a discussion on one of our podcasts, Dan confessed to repeatedly returning to the bar to fetch her glass after glass of white wine. I joked that he was an enabler, but the truth is he was just fetching booze for everyone. The sports medicine personnel were not happy about the idea of sending Carol home alone. Dan had wandered off at this point, and I realized it was up to me to make sure Carol made it back to her flat in Kensington safe and sound. I gamely volunteered to escort her, mostly because I felt responsible for her fall, but also because I genuinely liked Carol. She had been nothing but kind and warm to Dan, Dean, and me, and this was not the way I wanted her Olympic experience to end.

It took us a while to hail a cab since it was the night of the closing ceremony, but we finally flagged one down and Carol managed to slur her address coherently enough for the driver to understand. The entire ride consisted of me answering the same three questions over and over:

"Did any of the other crew see what happened?" [No.]

"Will you tell anyone?" [No.]

"I swear on the Holy Bible this has never happened before. Do you believe me?" [No. But I will gladly say yes if you stop asking the same three questions.]

As we drove through the streets on my final night in London, I couldn't help but think this was probably an appropriate way for my Olympic experience to end. I had complained about my role, not getting what I thought I deserved, and in the end I got exactly what I deserved: escorting the drunkest woman in the drunkest city on the planet back to her flat with absolutely no chance of sex as a reward. Karma is a bitch.

When we finally arrived at Carol's flat, I asked the driver if he would mind waiting a few minutes so I could escort her up the steps to her door. He agreed and we began to exit the cab, at which point I realized Carol couldn't walk on her own. She draped her arm around my shoulder, and I basically dragged her across her quiet Kensington side street to her front door. She managed to find her keys, but once we were inside she informed me there was no elevator. "Which floor are you on?" I asked.

"Free," she replied. I guess that meant three. This was going to be a challenge.

Have you ever dragged a lifeless body up two flights of stairs? I don't recommend it, but that was the task in front of me that night.

"I'm fine. Honestly!" pleaded Carol.

Good luck. The woman couldn't even climb a stepladder by herself much less navigate two flights. She once again draped her arm around me, and I pulled her up the creaky, old steps. The building was very old and the stairway was very narrow, making it very likely the toughest workout I had experienced in three years.

Step by step we made our climb, Carol continuing to ask the same three questions the entire time, genuinely fearful she had somehow done damage to her career. The only damage she was doing was to my back.

Finally, we made it to her front door. Wobbly, barely holding her up, exhausted, sweating out the alcohol I had consumed, but we had made it. She teetered beside me as she once again fumbled with her purse in search of the key to her door. At that moment, she stopped and looked up at me with puppy dog eyes. I expected her to begin a long, rambling, and incoherent speech about how grateful she was that I had taken her all this way and made sure she was safe. How I was a true gentleman for following through and putting her safety ahead of my enjoyment on this final evening in one of the world's great cities. I looked into her eyes. She opened her mouth and said, "I wish Dean were here."

↯

The next day as I went to check out of the hotel, I knew I still had the matter of the vomit-stained sheets and mattress bill to settle up. One hundred and twenty pounds worth. Wandering through the hotel lobby, I managed to track down the hotel manager, the one who'd sent me the third and final letter.

It had been a full two weeks since the incident, two weeks of the Olympic Games, two weeks of late nights in the hotel bar, where the bartenders and waitresses knew us by name. Where the concept of ordering a "double double" became a nightly normalcy—a "double double" in this case being four shots of gin, a splash of delicious English tonic, and a squeeze of lime. Two weeks of us unwinding in the pit of the hotel on a nightly basis and charging a good chunk of the bills back to our own rooms. It took a moment to jog his memory.

He printed out my room charges and soon remembered who I was: "There's nothing I can do for you, sir; the mattress and sheets were damaged."

"Take a closer look at the bill," I said.

He took a closer look at the grand total of my debauchery, of our mark on the city of London, of a wonderful trip and a wonderful life experience, and his eyebrows raised.

"We'll drop the charges; have a nice trip."

AFTERWORD

Enoteca Drago in Beverly Hills isn't exactly the kind of place the paparazzi camp out in front of every day. I'm sure at one point the Italian restaurant was an L.A. hot spot, especially right after *Rocky IV* was released (I can only assume the establishment was named after the Russian arch-nemesis in that film, played by Dolph Lundgren). However, on this Monday night in early July of 2013, it was practically empty, save for a gathering of new employees of Fox Sports 1.

When Fox executives had first contacted me almost exactly a year previously, I wasn't exactly thinking about a move south, I was thinking about coming home. Our time at the London Olympics was swiftly coming to a close, we had caused a bit of trouble—or should I say *I* had caused a bit of trouble with my various shenanigans, including my skin-tight full-body Union Jack unitard—and I was now eager to return home and resume another year of the Kraft Celebration Tour, an event where I could get on stage with Dan in front of thousands of adoring *SportsCentre* fans and sing songs while spending nights in small-town bars across the country having too many shots and generally having a great time.

"Would you ever consider coming to work in the United States?" they had asked.

I *had* considered it, years ago, when I was first starting out. In fact, just before I got that first on-air job in Saskatoon in 1998 I was offered another on-air job, in a *tiny* Oregon town for a tiny ABC affiliate that had just hired a brand new news director who probably wasn't much older than me. I had seen an online ad on tvspy.com for a weekend sports anchor position, and I mailed them a demo tape, hoping perhaps they might like me so much they would consider going through the trouble of hiring immigration lawyers and getting me a U.S. work visa. The young news director did indeed like my tape, and he called to offer me a job. I was elated until I asked him about that U.S. work visa.

"You don't need a U.S. work visa, right?" was his reply.

"Pretty sure I do," I sheepishly said.

"Oh, okay. Let me look into it and call you right back," he said.

I never heard from him again.

I never thought about the United States much after that, especially once Dan and I started to enjoy some real success in our own country. People would ask us about going to the States all the time, and our answer was always the same: They won't let us be "us" down there; they stopped doing that at ESPN in the Keith Olbermann, Dan Patrick, and Craig Kilborn days. Now the *SportsCenter* anchors were for the most part straight-shooting professional broadcasters, not guys who dressed up like the Phantom of the Opera. Besides, we loved hockey, and ESPN was pretty much ignoring the NHL at that point. No, we reasoned, we were just fine in Canada, thanks.

Then BlackBerry started falling apart, and everything changed.

The Canadian company that made BlackBerry mobile devices was in serious trouble by 2012. So much trouble that the *Wall Street Journal* saw fit to station one of their American reporters in Toronto because they were doing so many stories about the floundering smartphone empire. That reporter turned out to be Will Connors, a Chicago native and huge sports fan who turned on the

TV one morning to catch highlights on what he thought was a carbon copy of the American *SportsCenter* (albeit with the Canadian spelling), only to be awakened by what he described as "a loopier, freer-flowing affair." He became a regular viewer and approached TSN about doing a story in the *Wall Street Journal* about Dan and me. Will came to the studio in Scarborough to watch a live show and interview us, and the story came out a few weeks later. It was titled "Why Can't We Have Canada's '*SportsCentre*'?"

Careful what you wish for.

Around that same time, Fox Sports executives had decided to mount their own challenge to ESPN. NBC and CBS had recently launched their own brand new sports networks. Turns out sports television in 2012 was a very hot commodity. With cable companies fighting illegal online pirating and streaming, sports kept people paying for their cable bills by virtue of the fact that sports television was just about the only form of the medium that was "DVR proof." Sports are meant to be seen live. Sure you can DVR your favourite game and watch it later, but in this day and age of social media and smartphones, the chances of keeping the result from being spoiled for you is pretty slim. Not to mention the fact that sports are also always better on a big screen. You might not mind tearing through five seasons of *The Wire* on your laptop or tablet, but sports are always more fun to watch with others, on a big screen, with plenty of food and drink at the ready. Suddenly sports leagues were cashing in from major competition among the networks for rights fees to show the biggest live games, and now Fox wanted in, and they wanted to be different.

Fox had made the decision to do something slightly more unconventional than your standard two guys (or girls) in suits highlight show, and just as they had made the decision to do so, one of their executives picked up a copy of that day's *Wall Street Journal* with a headline that said "Why Can't We Have Canada's '*SportsCentre*'?"

The courtship lasted about a year. Fox started recording our show out of their Fox Soccer Channel studios in Vancouver, and they liked what they saw. They also heard us repeatedly reference Producer Tim and decided they wanted him as part of the package as well. Their pitch: to literally pick up our show from Toronto and move it to Los Angeles. The most appealing part might have been the time zone change. Suddenly instead of returning home at 2:30 a.m. we would be returning home at 11:30 p.m. We might even be able to go for a drink after the show.

More than the late-night drinking possibilities, Fox addressed our biggest concern about a move away from our comfort zone north of the 49th parallel: They were looking for an alternative to ESPN, and they didn't want to change us. They wanted us to be us.

As I was wrestling with the decision, I happened upon an interview in the *Globe and Mail* with Kelly Oxford, the Edmonton-born writer who had just published a book of essays titled *Everything Is Perfect When You're a Liar* (also published by HarperCollins; you're welcome HarperCollins!). Oxford had just uprooted her family, including her husband and three children, from Calgary to Los Angeles for greater career opportunities. She described it as an extremely difficult decision, but in the end, her husband was quoted in the article as saying, "When we're 75, living in Canada, we'll think, why didn't we try it? We could have just gone down there and checked it out."

Obviously as I struggled with the very same decision, these words struck a chord, not to mention the fact that the winter of 2012 was *really friggin' cold*.

When we announced that we were leaving, the outpouring of support, despair, and anger was fairly overwhelming. To some we were sellouts, chasing American cash and glory like so many opportunistic Canadians before us. To others we were abandoning a legion of loyal viewers who had grown up with us, just as Mark

Milliere had said they would all those years ago when he first put us on in the morning. Then there were those who were just happy for us to get the opportunity to ply our trade to a wider audience. We even got a tweet from the prime minister of Canada, Stephen Harper, complete with a picture of the three of us together at the 2012 Grey Cup, calling our move "The Worst Play of the Day" but wishing us well.

As I have detailed in this book, this job is all about moving from place to place, never getting complacent, always moving onward and upward for that new challenge. I had honestly thought those days were behind me. I was ready to settle in for another solid decade of fun at TSN with Dan.

Then I remembered how excited I was to get that first job in Saskatoon in '98. I had so much doubt about leaving Toronto back then. I had just as much doubt about leaving Toronto now. But in a way, that's what made it so appealing: the uncertainty. I didn't get in this business to play it safe. I could have stayed in Athabasca at the drugstore if I had wanted that.

Two months after it was announced we were leaving (which may have been the longest goodbye in Canadian television history), Dan, Producer Tim, and I joined our fellow new employees of Fox Sports 1 at Enoteca Drago for dinner and a bit of a meet and greet.

Fox had been incredibly good to us to that point, putting us up in temporary housing right by the beach in Santa Monica and assigning someone to practically hold my hand and take me to the DMV to get my California driver's licence. I was happy to meet my new colleagues, but I was dreading what the night was about to bring. I had sworn to another fellow Canadian import, Julie Stewart-Binks, a Toronto girl who had recently been hired by FS1 from CTV Regina, that if our new bosses asked us to get up in front of everyone and introduce ourselves like we were at summer camp, I would walk out of there. Just get up and walk out of the restaurant. I could not bear the idea of having to stand up and bare my soul like it was some sort of AA meeting. I would rather have someone rip my eyelashes out.

But sure enough, after a round of appetizers and some small talk among my fellow diners, my new boss, Scott Ackerson, got up and announced that we would indeed be going around the room one by one to introduce ourselves and bare our souls like it was some sort of AA meeting. He was standing right at the door. There was no chance of sneaking away unnoticed. I was trapped, and my biggest nightmare was about to come to fruition.

Thankfully I didn't have to go first. Some of my fellow on-air personalities from our new show *Fox Sports Live* as well as our new producers were up first. Included in this group was former NBA defensive player of the year Gary Payton, who informed us he had recently been divorced and would not be getting married again. I laughed because I was just months away from getting married for the second time, something I once swore I would never do again. Next up was fellow FS1 panelist and recently retired U.S. tennis star Andy Roddick, an athlete I once called out on-air for his treatment of referees and umpires during matches. I thought he would be a pretentious jerk. Turns out he was just the opposite. The second I shook his hand, I thought the same thing I once thought with Jon Ljungberg: "I will get along with this person. This person and I will be friends." He was hilarious and totally self-deprecating, talking about spending his career as "Federer's bitch" and wearing hats to cover up bald spots.

Another fellow FS1 panelist, Donovan McNabb, treated the event like he was giving a speech to a Fortune 500 company, speaking eloquently about becoming a team and battling the competition. He spoke clearly and confidently, and I felt like running a marathon when he was done. I was feeling good about the new panel on our show, but there were only a few more employees before I would have to get up and tell the entire room about myself.

Earlier in the day, when I was discussing the possibility of this very moment with Dan, he made a suggestion that I say something outlandish. He was joking, but I was desperate, and I *did* do something pretty outlandish that day. My turn was up. I swallowed another forkful of arugula salad, stood up, and spoke.

"I told Julie Stewart-Binks that if I had to get up and speak at this dinner, I would walk out of this fucking room."

Uproarious laughter.

"The only reason I didn't is because Scott is standing at the door."

Uproarious laughter continues. And then . . .

"I love being on television, but I hate speaking in front of people. I am a sports anchor—I'm really only comfortable in front of the camera."

I looked over at Dan. Then I paused, looked up, and addressed the entire room:

"So I masturbated several times today so I would feel relaxed and comfortable."

The room practically keeled over.

And so begins the next step of the journey.

ACKNOWLEDGEMENTS

I CAN'T BEGIN THE ACKNOWLEDGEMENTS with anyone other than my beautiful wife. She allowed me to skip out on many a beautiful Saturday afternoon we would otherwise have spent together, so I could finish this book. She also read the manuscript in its early stages and not only offered great suggestions but also likely kept me from being sued. If my career itself wasn't already evidence that I am a lucky man, then having her by my side is concrete proof. Every day I spend with her is a great day, especially if that day happens to take place at Disneyland.

Speaking of reading the manuscript in its early stages, I must also thank two of my best friends in the world, Peter Sayn-Wittgenstein and Piya Chattopadhyay, for also trudging through early versions of this book and giving me concrete advice about how to make it better. Look for Peter to write a book much better than this one when he is finished watching that Corbin Bernsen mini-series on his PVR. Piya, you are the best export Saskatchewan ever produced.

My brilliant and beautiful literary agent, Carly Watters, is most responsible for the book you have in your hands today. She was the one who suggested that getting off my ass and putting pen to paper might be a good idea. Carly, you have been amazing through this entire process, and I am forever grateful. I am also not weirded out by the fact that you look pretty much exactly like my ex-wife.

My brilliant and beautiful editor at HarperCollins, Doug Richmond, is someone I hope I can maintain a working relationship with my entire life. If I had literally hand-picked an editor, I couldn't have ended up with anyone so perfect. Thanks for your long and detailed e-mails, Doug. I am also not weirded out by the fact that you look a lot like Jonathan Franzen.

Thanks to designer Greg Tabor, photographer Kathryn Hollinrake and makeup artist Christine Cho for the fantastic cover.

Also thanks to the entire staff at HarperCollins, including Patricia MacDonald, Barbara Kamienski, Kelly Hope, Emma Ingram, Jason Pratt and Shannon Parsons, for making me feel so welcome and a part of the family.

Speaking of family, thanks once again to my parents, who were pretty much dealing with a weirdo the second I was born but continued to trudge on anyway. Also thanks to the rest of the Onrait clan: My sister, Erin, who can whip up a mean apple juice and ham casserole at the drop of a hat. My brother-in-law, Trevor, who is better than me at every single sport we try and never gloats about it. My niece, Brooklyn, and my nephews, Noah and Keaton, always make me laugh and bring me joy. My grandfather, Rene, who gave me a 1970 Buick Skylark for my sixteenth birthday, thereby making him the coolest man alive.

Thanks to my good friend and longtime co-anchor, Dan O'Toole, for talking me off the ledge more times than I can remember and for contributing a brilliant foreword to this book. Well, "brilliant" may be a stretch, but he got it done and the jury was out on that one. Thanks also to our longtime producer and good friend, Producer Tim, for very likely saving our jobs several times over the last ten years and joining us on this new adventure to California.

Thanks to all my wonderful employers past and present, especially Mark Milliere, Ken Volden, Phil King, Stewart Johnston, and Keith Pelley at TSN; Darcy Modin at A-Channel; Lisa Ford at Global Saskatoon; Pat Kiernan at ITV Edmonton; and my dad, who was forced to employ me at his drugstore because my mom told him to. Thanks also to all my fellow employees at TSN over the years who provided me with great fodder for storytelling and many laughs along the way.

Thanks to the entire staff at Dark Horse Espresso Bar on Spadina Avenue between Queen Street and Dundas Street in Toronto, where I wrote almost every single word of this book like I was some wannabe screenwriter. This includes owners Ed Lynds and Deanna Zunde and hard-working employees Ryan Kukec, Maxine Gagnon, Rob Hasebe, Rob Piron, Phil Cox, Danny Flynn, Becky Weekes, Lisa D'Allessandro, Momi Kishi, Otillo Page, Batouli Baccar, Axel Steingrimigson, and Dave Metcalfe, who served me about 3,000 jasmine green teas and Americanos over the course of a year. They also played some great tunes while I tried to pound out my 2,000 words a day in accordance with Stephen King's *On Writing*. If you're ever wandering around Toronto's Chinatown, this is *the* place to stop and rest and people-watch.

Finally a special thanks to all the viewers who have said such kind things to me on Twitter and in person over the course of the past few years. I hope you enjoy this book, and I hope Canadians don't hold it against me that I left for the United States. I will always be a proud Canadian.